Top Speed

CARS

Kane Miller
A DIVISION OF EDC PUBLISHING

Pagani Huayra BC

First American Edition 2019
Kane Miller, A Division of EDC Publishing

For information contact:
Kane Miller, A Division of EDC Publishing
P.O. Box 470663
Tulsa, OK 74147-0663
www.kanemiller.com
www.edcpub.com
www.usbornebooksandmore.com

Library of Congress Control Number: 2018958527
ISBN: 978-1-61067-904-6

Despite extensive research of current sources,
performance and economy figures for cars can vary due
to inconsistency and local variables in testing methods.
Sometimes, figures are estimates or simply not available.
Picture credits

FC: Bugatti. p1 (tl) Aston Martin Lagonda; (tr) Dodge; (bl)
Mercedes-Benz (Daimler AG); (br) Nissan Motor Co. p2–3
Pagani Automobili SpA. p4–5 Spyker NV. p6–7 Mercedes-
Benz (Daimler AG). p8–9 Mini (BMW). p18–19 Mercedes-
Benz (Daimler AG). p30–31 BMW. p42–43 BAC. p52–53
Mercedes-Benz (Daimler AG). p66–67 Alfa Romeo (FCA).
p82–83 Jaguar Land Rover. p96–97 Dodge (FCA). p110–111
Ferrari SpA.

All remaining pictures are copyright of the relevant model's
motor manufacturer: Alfa Romeo (FCA), Abarth & C SpA
(FCA), Ariel Motor Co, Aston Martin Lagonda Ltd,
Automobili Lamborghini SpA, Audi AG and UK, BAC (Briggs
Automotive Co), Bentley Motors Ltd, BMW AG and UK,
Bugatti, Cadillac, Caparo plc, Caterham Cars, Chevrolet,
Dodge (FCA), Elemental Motor Co Ltd, Ferrari SpA, Fiat
Automobiles (FCA), Ford Motor Co, GM (General Motors),
Hennessey Performance Engineering, Holden Australia,
Honda Motor Co, ItalDesign Giugiaro SpA, Jaguar Land
Rover, Jeep (FCA), Koenigsegg Automotive AB, KTM AG,
Lexus, Lotus Group, Maserati SpA (FCA), Mazda Motor
Corp, McLaren Automotive, Mercedes-Benz (Daimler AG),
Mini (BMW), Morgan Motor Co, NIO, Nissan Motor Co Ltd,
Pagani Automobili SpA, Peugeot/Group PSA, Porsche AG
and UK, Opel Automobile GmgH, Radical Sportscars,
Groupe Renault, Rolls-Royce Motor Cars (BMW), Scuderia
Cameron Glickenhaus LLC, Seat SA, smart Automobile
(Daimler AG), Spyker NV, TechRules, Tesla Inc, Vanda
Electrics Pte Ltd, Vauxhall Motors UK, Volkswagen Group,
Volvo Car Corporation and Zenvo Automotive AS.

Printed and bound in Malaysia, December 2020
2 3 4 5 6 7 8 9 10

TOP SPEED

CARS

100 EXTREME MACHINES

Small aileron and low-drag air inlet on the Spyker C8 Preliator supercar.

Contents

It was three-time drivers' world champion Sir Jackie Stewart, who coined the nickname "Green Hell" for the Nordschleife, a circuit at the old race track at Nürburgring, Germany. Consisting of 12.9 miles and 73 turns, steep inclines, and tricky corners, manufacturers target their fastest cars (and drivers!) with achieving the fastest lap time. The result: breathtaking speeds from many *Top Speed* cars.

Taking a corner on the Nordschleife in a Nürburgring star, the Mercedes-AMG GT R.

Time	Car	Year
6 mins 43.22 secs	McLaren P1 GTR LM	2017
6 mins 45.90 secs	NextEV NIO EP9	2017
6 mins 48.00 secs	Radical SR8LM	2009
6 mins 52.01 secs	Lamborghini Huracan Performante	2017
6 mins 57.00 secs	Porsche 918 Spyder	2013
6 mins 59.73 secs	Lamborghini Aventador LP750-4 Superveloce	2015
7 mins 03.45 secs	Dodge Viper SRT-10 ACR Extreme	2017
7 mins 08.68 secs	Nissan GT-R Nismo	2015
7 mins 10.92 secs	Mercedes-AMG GT R	2017
7 mins 12.70 secs	Porsche 911 GT3	2017
7 mins 16.00 secs	Chevrolet Camaro ZL1 1LE	2017
7 mins 21.63 secs	Ferrari 488 GTB	2015
7 mins 27.88 secs	BMW M4 GTS	2016
7 mins 32.00 secs	Alfa Romeo Giulia Quadrifoglio	2016
7 mins 32.19 secs	Ford Shelby GT350R	2015
7 mins 38.00 secs	Porsche Panamera Turbo	2017
7 mins 43.80 secs	Honda Civic Type R	2017
7 mins 47.19 secs	Volkswagen Golf GTI Clubsport S	2016
7 mins 54.36 secs	Renault Mégane RS 275 Trophy-R	2015
7 mins 59.74 secs	Porsche Cayenne Turbo S	2016

Source: https://nurburglaptimes.com

Pocket Rockets

▶ A pocket rocket is a small car that has big ambitions – high top speed, great handling, and really fast acceleration. Turbocharging means even tiny engines can deliver big power, while upgraded brakes and fat tires guarantee they stop as well as they go. At heart, they might be the same as other models in their range with much less power, but a true pocket rocket will always stand out. Alloy wheels, spoilers, a spine-tingling exhaust note, and even racing stripes, play their part in making these rockets roar!

RenaultSport Clio 220 Trophy

Country of manufacture	France	Starting at $29,000

Few companies know as much about making a pocket rocket go – and handle beautifully – as RenaultSport. They have come up with classics over the years, and the latest is uprated in all the right places to be a bundle of fun on twisty roads. Purists bemoan the paddle-shift automatic, but there's Race mode and Launch control...

The facelifted front end of this Clio has new headlights that will light up the night with nine LEDs and six reflectors. Also note the checkered-flag-inspired pattern on the bumper. Nice touch!

 Performance

Top speed	146 mph
0–62 mph	6.6 secs
Power	220 hp
Torque	206 lb-ft

 Engine

Capacity	1.6-liter 4 cylinder
Type	Turbocharged

 Efficiency

Mileage	47.9 mpg

 Dimensions

Curb weight	2,665 lb
Power/weight	166 hp/ton
Length	160 in

Mini John Cooper Works

Country of manufacture	United Kingdom	Starting at $31,000

Minis aren't as mini as they used to be, but they are just as sporty! The quickest is the John Cooper Works. It gets a bigger 2.0-liter engine than the 1.6 Cooper S, sports suspension, and a choice of manual or auto transmission. We suggest the paddle-shift auto: it's two-tenths of a second quicker than the manual 'box!

Spot this badge on the front of a Mini, and you'll know it's fast! "Works" was the name of the heated-up Mini Coopers of the 1960s.

 Performance

Top speed	153 mph
0–62 mph	6.1 secs
Power	231 hp
Torque	236 lb-ft

 Engine

Capacity	2.0-liter 4 cylinder
Type	Turbocharged

 **Efficiency**

Mileage	49.6 mpg

 **Dimensions**

Curb weight	2,885 lb
Power/weight	162 hp/ton
Length	152.5 in

Audi S1 quattro Competition

Country of manufacture	Belgium	Starting at $36,000

It may be Audi's smallest car, but there's nothing junior about the S1 quattro, especially in sporty Competition form. It is as at home in day-to-day driving as it is sprinting around a circuit, and quattro all-wheel drive means it can do it all, rain or shine. With the Golf GTI engine and a six-speed manual gearbox, it's a mini-beast!

Sporty five-spoke wheels do a good job setting off S1's design – and a great job showing off the smallest Audi's red-painted brake calipers!

Performance

Top speed	155 mph
0–62 mph	5.8 secs
Power	231 hp
Torque	273 lb-ft

Engine

Capacity	2.0-liter 4 cylinder
Type	Turbocharged

Efficiency

Mileage	39.8 mpg

Dimensions

Curb weight	2,900 lb
Power/weight	221 hp/ton
Length	156.5 in

Vauxhall/Opel Corsa VXR

Countries of manufacture	Germany and Spain	Starting at $23,500

The hottest little Vauxhall/Opel pocket rocket used to wear Nürburgring badges, which tells you something about its performance aspirations. The badge may be no more – it's just plain Corsa VXR now – but all the good parts of the 'Ring pack are present: 205-hp turbo 1.6 motor, lowered suspension, and Recaro seats.

Even though not the fastest anymore, the VXR is a driver's delight. Its baseball-sized shift knob and pocket-rocket dials can be admired from the Recaro sports seats that will hold you rock steady during cornering.

 Performance

Top speed	143 mph
0–62 mph	6.8 secs
Power	205 hp
Torque	206 lb-ft

 Engine

Capacity	1.6-liter 4 cylinder
Type	Turbocharged

 **Efficiency**

Mileage	37.7 mpg

 **Dimensions**

Curb weight	2,818 lb
Power/weight	145 hp/ton
Length	158.9 in

Smart Fortwo Brabus

Country of manufacture | **France**   **Starting at $27,500**

Brabus is famous for 900-hp Merc conversions and other specials that rank among the world's fastest conversions. The German tuning firm also waves its performance wand over this: a tiny city car with a 900-cc three-cylinder engine in the back. It's the Smart Fortwo, and while it only has 109 hp, it does have Race Start mode!

It might have half the power of other pocket rockets, but the Brabus isn't short on attitude – inside or outside.

Performance

Top speed	103 mph
0–62 mph	9.5 secs
Power	109 hp
Torque	125 lb-ft

Engine

Capacity	900-cc 3 cylinder
Type	Turbocharged

Efficiency

Mileage	62.8 mpg

Dimensions

Curb weight	2194 lb
Power/weight	99 hp/ton
Length	107.9 in

Volkswagen Polo GTI

Country of manufacture	Spain		Starting at $28,000

The VW Polo is growing up! After 14 million cars and five generations, it's certainly time. The all-new GTI, with 2.0-liter TSI engine and 200 hp, promises to be the sportiest Polo ever. The same size as a 2004 Golf, it has a digital dashboard, GTI-style trim, and either six-speed manual or seven-speed DSG transmission.

New MkVI Polo GTI ditches the previous 1.8-liter engine for the more powerful 2.0-liter turbo.

 Performance

Top speed	147 mph*
0–62 mph	6.7 secs*
Power	200 hp
Torque	184 lb-ft*

 Engine

Capacity	2.0-liter 4 cylinder
Type	Turbocharged

 **Efficiency**

Mileage	50.4 mpg*

 **Dimensions**

Curb weight	2,822 lb*
Power/weight	142 hp/ton*
Length	159.6 in

Note: * = figures for 1.8 version; new model details not available.

Ford Fiesta ST200

Country of manufacture | **Global sites** | **Starting at $29,500**

Keen drivers the world over have decided: for all-around ability, the ST200 is a five-star champion. There are faster pocket rockets, but probably none that handle as sweetly or come with as few compromises for everyday use – quite a claim, even for a car like Fiesta, with so many revered hot versions over the years.

Carbon-fiber dashboard inserts, alloy-metal pedals and gearshift, and an ST-specification steering wheel are just a few of the ST200's home comforts. But don't get too comfy – there's a new Fiesta ready to roll out of the factory!

 Performance

Top speed	143 mph
0–62 mph	6.7 secs
Power	200 hp
Torque	214 lb-ft

 Engine

Capacity	1.6-liter 4 cylinder
Type	Turbocharged

 **Efficiency**

Mileage	46.3 mpg

 **Dimensions**

Curb weight	3473 lb
Power/weight	115 hp/ton
Length	156.8 in

Abarth 695 Biposto

Country of manufacture	Italy	Starting at $43,000

Italians love small cars, and they love motor racing – put them together and you get the 695 Biposto. It's a Fiat 500 two-seater and the closest thing you can get to a mini race car for the road. With Brembo brakes, adjustable suspension, racing gearbox, and more, it's top Italian *brio* – with a great exhaust note to boot!

The "Abarth Corsa by Sabelt" special edition, with its four-point seat belts, polycarbonate windows, OZ wheels, and titanium wheel bolts, is so race spec that you might feel underdressed behind the wheel without an Arai helmet.

 Performance

Top speed	143 mph
0–62 mph	5.9 secs
Power	190 hp
Torque	184 lb-ft

Engine

Capacity	1.4-liter 4 cylinder
Type	Turbocharged

 Efficiency

Mileage	45.6 mpg

 **Dimensions**

Curb weight	2198 lb
Power/weight	173 hp/ton
Length	144 in

Hot Hatches

Inside every tame family hatchback lurks a rip-roaring sports machine! Three- or five-door hot hatchbacks, or sport compacts, existed before the 1976 VW Golf GTI, but this was the car that really put hot hatches on the map. And they haven't looked back since. Today they use turbochargers to extract huge horsepower from mostly four-cylinder engines, and with advanced suspensions and aerodynamics, they are faster than many sports cars — but still offer room for the family!

Nissan Juke-R 2.0

Country of manufacture	United Kingdom	Starting at $520,000

It's the maddest hot hatch ever – a Nissan Juke crossed with a Nissan GT-R supercar – with almost 600 hp and awesome acceleration! It started as a concept car, but some people had to have one, whatever it cost. Under the wild body it is all GT-R, including all-wheel drive – which it definitely needs with all that power!

Performance

Top speed	160 mph plus
0–60 mph	3.3 secs
Power	592 hp
Torque	481 lb-ft

Engine

Capacity	3.8-liter V6
Type	Twin turbocharged

Efficiency

Mileage	Not available

Dimensions

Curb weight	Not available
Power/weight	Not available
Length	Not available

Twin rear carbon-fiber winglets make a very purposeful addition to the Juke-R's style – as well as creating some downforce at speed. And speed is what this thing's all about! This car is so specialized, many details are kept under wraps.

Ford Focus RS

| **Country of manufacture** | **Germany** | **Starting at $41,120** |

RS is Ford's recipe for driving bliss. But with more power than ever, something had to be done to keep this wild child from misbehaving. So the handling has been tamed with all-wheel drive, making it much more usable on all roads. There's even a Drift button – here's a 4x4 hot hatch that can oversteer like a muscle car.

Body-hugging Recaro seats and a manual gearbox are icing on the Focus RS cake. And did you know that Ford's "engine listeners" check each 2.3-liter unit to make sure the 320-hp engine is in the peak of good health?

 Performance

Top speed	165 mph
0–62 mph	4.7 secs
Power	320 hp
Torque	347 lb-ft

 Engine

Capacity	2.3-liter 4 cylinder
Type	Turbocharged

 **Efficiency**

Mileage	36.7 mpg

 **Dimensions**

Curb weight	3,411 lb
Power/weight	188 hp/ton
Length	172.8 in

RenaultSport Mégane 275 Trophy-R

Country of manufacture	France	Starting at $37,500

The first front-driver to break eight minutes at the Nürburgring in 2014, the Trophy-R is the ultimate Mégane. The R (two seats and full roll cage) is a limited edition, but the regular Trophy has the same 275 horses. In 2017, an all-new version brings four-wheel steering and a choice of manual or paddle-shift dual-clutch gearbox.

Alloy pedals and white-faced dials do their best to sportify the Mégane's now-dated interior. The new version will improve things, and gets paddle-shift auto as well as manual gearbox. It will be out to get its 'Ring record back!

 Performance

Top speed	158 mph
0–62 mph	5.8 secs
Power	275 hp
Torque	265 lb-ft

 Engine

Capacity	2.0-liter 4 cylinder
Type	Turbocharged

 Efficiency

Mileage	37.7 mpg

 Dimensions

Curb weight	2,860 lb
Power/weight	192 hp/ton
Length	170.5 in

Seat Leon SC CUPRA R

CUPRA has long been Spanish for sporty Seats, and the spicier the better. The Leon SC is the hottest of them all – with 300 hp, it's the most powerful Seat ever. It comes in both front-drive and (in the ST wagon version) all-wheel drive forms, and also with a choice of body styles and either manual or paddle-shift auto 'boxes.

The checkered flag badge is not just for show: this Spanish flyer was honed at the Nürburgring. Seat offers lots of model choice – all with a tasty 300 hp!

 Performance

Top speed	155 mph
0–62 mph	5.6 secs
Power	300 hp
Torque	280 lb-ft

 Engine

Capacity	2.0- liter 4 cylinder
Type	Turbocharged

 **Efficiency**

Mileage	42.2 mpg

 **Dimensions**

Curb weight	3,076 lb
Power/weight	195 hp/ton
Length	167.2 in

Honda Civic Type R

Country of manufacture	United Kingdom	Starting at $35,595

"Type R" is part of hot hatch legend. The sporty Civic in its most powerful form reinvented the breed in the 1990s, captivating fans who were distraught when Honda stopped making it. Now the winged wonder is back, and the latest 2018 version is setting the pace. Turbocharged and with front-wheel drive, it'll do almost 170 mph!

It's a mix of vents, scoops, strakes, wings, bumps and edges, and even a triple bazooka exhaust. Vortex generators at the roof's back edge channel airflow toward the Type R's huge rear wing.

 Performance

Top speed	169 mph
0–62 mph	5.8 secs
Power	320 hp
Torque	295 lb-ft

Engine

Capacity	2.0-liter 4 cylinder
Type	Turbocharged

 Efficiency

Mileage	36.7 mpg

 Dimensions

Curb weight	3,043 lb
Power/weight	210 hp/ton
Length	179.4 in

Peugeot 308 GTi

Country of manufacture	France		Starting at $38,000

If VW's Golf was the first hot hatch, then Peugeot's influential 205 GTi of the 1980s is usually considered the best. Fast and agile, it could be a handful in the corners, but get it right and the rewards were immense. Also fast and agile, but in no way a handful, is today's hot Pug. The 308 GTi is a talented all-arounder.

GTi by name, GTi by nature: the latest hot 308 marks a return to form for the French firm – even if one of the options for the car is the odd "Coupe Franche" two-color paint job.

 Performance

Top speed	155 mph
0–60 mph	6.0 secs
Power	272 hp
Torque	243 lb-ft

Engine

Capacity	1.6-liter 4 cylinder
Type	Turbocharged

 Efficiency

Mileage	47.1 mpg

 **Dimensions**

Curb weight	2,657 lb
Power/weight	205 hp/ton
Length	167.4 in

BMW M140i

Country of manufacture	Germany	Starting at $45,500

BMW's baby M car is the M2, a sedan. If you want a hatch, and a hot one, it has to be this. The M140i has a big engine for a small car and goes for smooth delivery more than outright power, but even so, it is delightfully fast and refined, with handing to die for. Plus, it makes one of the best noises in all of motoring!

BMW's M140i is a bit of a sleeper to look at, but it can really light up your drive with its smooth six-cylinder power and rear-wheel drive handling. It's real old-school!

Performance

Top speed	155 mph
0–62 mph	4.8 secs
Power	340 hp
Torque	369 lb-ft

Engine

Capacity	3.0-liter 6 cylinder
Type	Turbocharged

 Efficiency

Mileage	36.2 mpg

 Dimensions

Curb weight	3,352 lb
Power/weight	203 hp/ton
Length	170.2 in

Mercedes-AMG A45

Country of manufacture	Germany	Starting at $58,500

Mercedes isn't the first name to come to mind where hot hatches are concerned. But the AMG A45 is certainly a hatchback, and with a mind-boggling 381 hp from just 2.0 liters, it is definitely hot! With all-wheel drive and lots of electronic stability systems, it can get its power down with precision yet still be fun to drive.

Always fast and fun, things get even more exciting (and louder!) when you push the Sport button. There's also a Sport Handling mode for when you want to hang the tail out.

Performance

Top speed	155 mph
0–62 mph	4.2 secs
Power	381 hp
Torque	350 lb-ft

Engine

Capacity	2.0-liter 4 cylinder
Type	Turbocharged

 Efficiency

Mileage	40.9 mpg

 Dimensions

Curb weight	3,429 lb
Power/weight	222 hp/ton
Length	169.3 in

VW Golf GTI Clubsport S

Country of manufacture	Germany	Starting at $39,000

The daddy of all hot hatches is scorching when in Clubsport S form. The most powerful GTI ever smashed the Nürburgring lap record for front-drive cars in 2016, and even comes with a special handling setting tailored to the 'Ring. And, the three-door, two-seater ultimate GTI is as much of a hit on public roads.

There are only seats up front in this GTI. Part of VW's weight-loss strategy was to lose the two back seats, but this Nürburgring driver doesn't seem to mind.

Performance

Top speed	165 mph
0–62 mph	5.9 secs
Power	310 hp
Torque	280 lb-ft

Engine

Capacity	2.0-liter 4 cylinder
Type	Turbocharged

Efficiency

Mileage	38.2 mpg

Dimensions

Curb weight	3,000 lb
Power/weight	207 hp/ton
Length	168 in

Audi RS3 quattro

Country of manufacture	Germany	Starting at $56,000

Turbocharged, four-wheel drive, and with an inline five-cylinder engine – it could be the original Audi quattro. While the new version still boasts the five-pot exhaust beat, it comes with twice the power! With the charismatic quick-shifting S-Tronic dual-clutch automatic transmission, its 400 hp makes it superfast.

The S-Tronic seven-speed dual-clutch transmission and permanent all-wheel drive transfer the power of the five cylinders to the wheels. The sportier the driving, the more torque hits the rear axle.

 Performance

Top speed	155 mph
0–62 mph	4.1 secs
Power	400 hp
Torque	354 lb-ft

 Engine

Capacity	2.5-liter 5 cylinder
Type	Turbocharged

 **Efficiency**

Mileage	34.0 mpg

 **Dimensions**

Curb weight	3,330 lb
Power/weight	240 hp/ton
Length	170.7 in

Speedy SUVs

▶ Welcome to the world of the performance giants! Sport utility vehicles grew out of the light truck segment, but there's nothing truck-like about these monsters. From humble 4x4 beginnings, SUVs, or crossovers, have grown into the largest, most powerful, luxurious, and expensive cars on the planet, with all-terrain capability and a feel-good factor that only sitting high above everyone else can give. All the big names are in – there's even a Rolls-Royce SUV on the way!

Audi SQ7

Country of manufacture	Slovakia	Starting at $92,000

Seven-seat diesel 4x4s aren't what they used to be...look at Audi's flagship Q7. The three-row family wagon's twin-turbo V8 diesel is boosted by an electric compressor to churn out big power and even more impressive torque. Sub-5.0 sec 0–62 mph acceleration is the order of the day, but this car can do almost 40 mpg!

The SQ7's badge holds the clue to its massive performance: V8T stands for a twin-turbo V8, but there's no gas here. This engine's a diesel!

 Performance

Top speed	155 mph
0–62 mph	4.9 secs
Power	435 hp
Torque	664 lb-ft

 Engine

Capacity	4.0-liter V8
Type	Twin turbocharged

 **Efficiency**

Mileage	39.2 mpg

 **Dimensions**

Curb weight	5,138 lb
Power/weight	169 hp/ton
Length	199.6 in

Jaguar F-Pace S

Country of manufacture	United Kingdom		Starting at $60,000

Combining all Jaguar's traditional strengths in one superlative design, the F-Pace has become the marque's biggest-selling model. With "just" 380 hp from the supercharged V6 in the S version, it's not as powerful as some, but then the 0–62 mph time of 5.5 secs does come with a fuel economy of a possible 32 mpg.

The F-Pace S is a compact five-seater with plenty of appeal, as well as a large dose of sports car DNA to keep the driver happy. And to remind you of its power, there's the 20-inch five-spoke alloy wheels, red brake calipers, and S badging.

 Performance

Top speed	155 mph
0–62 mph	5.5 secs
Power	380 hp
Torque	332 lb-ft

 Engine

Capacity	3.0-liter V6
Type	Supercharged

 **Efficiency**

Mileage	31.7 mpg

 **Dimensions**

Curb weight	4,104 lb
Power/weight	185 hp/ton
Length	186.3 in

Maserati Levante S

| Country of manufacture | Italy | Starting at $92,000 |

The "Maserati of SUVs" conjures up an image of exotic styling and sports car handling, and the Levante hardly disappoints. In size and power, the current range-topping S model doesn't go to the lengths of some rivals, but with a charismatic 430 hp from the twin-turbo V6, it goes well, sounds great, and has Italian heart.

Based on the 2011 Kubang concept car, the Levante is an SUV with real Italian heart in its beautiful design and finish. Maserati's famous Trident emblem is embossed into all the head restraints.

Performance

Top speed	164 mph
0–62 mph	5.2 secs
Power	430 hp
Torque	442 lb-ft

Engine

Capacity	3.0-liter V6
Type	Twin turbocharged

 Efficiency

Mileage	26 mpg

 Dimensions

Curb weight	4,650 lb
Power/weight	185 hp/ton
Length	197 in

Mercedes-Maybach G650 Landaulet

Country of manufacture	Germany	Starting at $530,000

This is one of the most unlikely SUV superstars. There have been luxurious and powerful versions of Merc's original 4x4 before, but nothing quite like this AMG version with open landaulet body. This extravagance boasts a biturbo V12 with 630 hp – and enough hard-core off-roading hardware to go anywhere!

A stretched wheelbase means lots of room in the back – even with the electrically adjustable seats from the S-Class fitted, and complete with massage function, of course! Only 99 of these Mercs are being built.

 Performance

Top speed	112 mph
0–62 mph	5.8 secs
Power	630 hp
Torque	738 lb-ft

 Engine

Capacity	6.0-liter V12
Type	Twin turbocharged

 Efficiency

Mileage	Not available

 Dimensions

Curb weight	6,615 lb (estimate)
Power/weight	190 hp/ton (estimate)
Length	210.4 in

Bentley Bentayga

Country of manufacture	United Kingdom	Starting at $253,500

It's the poshest name in SUVs by far! The Bentayga takes everything the brand is known for – including the mega 6.0-liter W12 engine – and puts it into a high-riding cocoon of the finest materials and handcrafted luxury. Performance is simply massive, while it will also handle off-road routes with ease.

The Bentayga is like entering a parallel universe of power and refinement – but be warned, taking your seat behind the steering wheel with its famous winged B badge doesn't come cheap – this is one of the world's most expensive cars.

 Performance

Top speed	187 mph
0–62 mph	4.0 secs
Power	608 hp
Torque	664 lb-ft

 Engine

Capacity	6.0-liter W12
Type	Twin turbocharged

 Efficiency

Mileage	21.6 mpg

 Dimensions

Curb weight	5,380 lb
Power/weight	226 hp/ton
Length	202.4 in

BMW X6 M

Country of manufacture	United States		Starting at $105,700

Coupe-type styling and performance combine in BMW's flagship SUV. It looks like a power hero and goes like one. An absolute flyer in a straight line, it also goes well around corners, thanks to its Motorsport-honed handling. Back seat passengers might not like it, but this is an SUV you can throw around like a sports car!

Dial M for Motorsport: the gear selector proudly displays the famous *M* logo that has distinguished so many "ultimate driving machines" in the past.

 Performance

Top speed	155 mph
0–62 mph	4.2 secs
Power	575 hp
Torque	553 lb-ft

 Engine

Capacity	4.4-liter V8
Type	Twin turbocharged

 Efficiency

Mileage	25.4 mpg

 Dimensions

Curb weight	4,265 lb
Power/weight	220 hp/ton
Length	193.3 in

Tesla Model X Performance

Country of manufacture	United States	Starting at $152,000

Tesla is surging on a wave of electric power. The Model X is billed as "the safest, fastest and most capable sport utility vehicle in history." It might not be as good off road as Land Rover or Jeep, but it's fast in P100D form. The Ludicrous mode unleashes all that performance with the violence of an extreme fairground ride!

Adding to Model X's brilliant craziness: its signature Falcon Wing rear doors. They make it easy to access the third row of seats, and less than a foot of clear space is needed on each side for the doors to move up and out of the way.

 Performance

Top speed	155 mph
0–62 mph	3.1 secs
Power	603 hp
Torque	713 lb-ft

 Engine

Capacity	100 kWh
Type	Dual electric motor

 **Efficiency**

Mileage	Not available

 **Dimensions**

Curb weight	5,378 lb
Power/weight	224 hp/ton
Length	198.9 in

Jeep Grand Cherokee Trackhawk

Country of manufacture	United States		Starting at $86,200

In a world of fast SUVs, the 2018 Trackhawk is *very* FAST – as fast, in fact, as a Lamborghini or Ferrari supercar. For a 2.4-ton family wagon that can go off road, its speed is astonishing. Its secret is under the hood: a supercharged 6.2-liter V8 called Hellcat, delivering 707 hp and making it the most powerful SUV ever!

 Performance

Top speed	180 mph
0–60 mph	3.5 secs
Power	707 hp
Torque	645 lb-ft

 Engine

Capacity	6.2-liter V8
Type	Supercharged

Hellcat is the name of this most powerful SUV's engine. Unleash all its 700-plus horsepower and this ultimate Grand Cherokee feels like it is about to take off!

 **Efficiency**

Mileage	Not available

 Dimensions

Curb weight	5,365 lb
Power/weight	264 hp/ton
Length	189 in

Porsche Cayenne Turbo S

Starting at $102,900

Few cars combine all the SUV ingredients as convincingly as the Cayenne in Turbo S form. Practical, spacious, and superbly built, its turbo gas V8 delivers performance and response to shame many a sports car. No surprise really – it's built by the same company that makes 911s, 918 Spyders, and 919 Hybrid Le Mans winners!

With this monster of a turbocharged V8 under the hood, the Cayenne is faster than some Porsche sports cars. The big SUV also outsells the sports cars!

 Performance

Top speed	176 mph
0–62 mph	4.1 secs
Power	570 hp
Torque	500 lb-ft

 Engine

Capacity	4.8-liter V8
Type	Twin turbocharged

 **Efficiency**

Mileage	24.6 mpg

 **Dimensions**

Curb weight	5,094 lb
Power/weight	224 hp/ton
Length	191.1 in

Land Rover Range Rover Sport SVR

Country of manufacture	United Kingdom	Starting at $131,500

Despite more rivals than ever, there remains only one true global icon of the luxury SUV, and that's the Range Rover. It is instantly recognizable and outstandingly capable, even when in the extreme 550 hp high-performance form of the storming SVR Range Rover Sport. Basically, it is just mega!

Since Range Rover's perfect shape first appeared in 1970 – it even went into the New York Museum of Modern Art! – it has evolved through successive generations into one of the best-loved cars on the road.

 Performance

Top speed	162 mph
0–62 mph	4.7 secs
Power	550 hp
Torque	501 lb-ft

Engine

Capacity	5-liter V8
Type	Supercharged

 Efficiency

Mileage	22.1 mpg

 **Dimensions**

Curb weight	5,144 lb
Power/weight	214 hp/ton
Length	191.8 in

Road and Track Heroes

No road-registerable car is more focused on track ability than these. They are not necessarily the most powerful cars, but they are among the lightest – and that gives them what every race car needs: the best possible power/weight ratio. Incredibly stiff structures and advanced suspension systems confer mechanical grip, while sophisticated aerodynamics ensure they are sucked down onto the road – with the result that they go around corners like nothing else in this book. And yes, you can still drive them to the store!

Caterham Seven 620R

Country of manufacture	United Kingdom		Starting at $69,000

Caterham is the original supercar slayer! For decades now, its take on the original Lotus 7 has thrilled on both road and track; the thrill likened to that of a high-performance motorbike. The 620R is the ultimate Caterham, and the first with a supercharged engine. Combined with light weight, it offers astonishing performance.

The 620R's carbon seats each feature four-point racing harnesses to hold you securely in place on a circuit – and it's only on a circuit that the 620R's massive performance can safely be used.

 Performance

Top speed	155 mph
0–60 mph	2.79 secs
Power	310 hp
Torque	219 lb-ft

 Engine

Capacity	2.0-liter 4 cylinder
Type	Supercharged

 Efficiency

Mileage	Not available

 Dimensions

Curb weight	1,202 lb
Power/weight	516 hp/ton
Length	122 in

BAC Mono

Country of manufacture	United Kingdom	Starting at $161,500

Created with the aim of making the purest driving experience going, the Mono doesn't even have a passenger seat! It is crafted out of carbon fiber, with a 2.5-liter engine and racing-style sequential gearbox. With its huge power-to-weight ratio and balance, it's a road car that can take apart a circuit like a real racer.

Exposed on either side of the hood are the race-spec pushrods of the Mono's twin-wishbone suspension. These give it F1-style grip, even though it doesn't have an F1-style front wing, which is illegal on any road car.

 Performance

Top speed	170 mph
0–62 mph	2.8 secs
Power	309 hp
Torque	227 lb-ft

 Engine

Capacity	2.5-liter 4 cylinder
Type	Naturally aspirated

 **Efficiency**

Mileage	42.2 mpg

 **Dimensions**

Curb weight	1,279 lb
Power/weight	483 hp/ton
Length	155.6 in

Radical RXC Turbo 600R

Country of manufacture	United Kingdom		Starting at $171,280

In just 20 years, the Radical has become the road and track machine to beat. Light, powerful, and with high downforce, the cars are virtually Le Mans racers for the road! In 2009, an SR8 was driven from the UK to the Nürburgring, where it set a record that stood for years. The 600R corners at 2g, putting the SR8 in the shade!

Inside the cockpit, accessed via the falcon-wing doors, there are Alcantara Radical embroidered Corbeau seats and Alcantara finish. On the dash of this special edition is a 20th anniversary plaque, marking the 2,000[th] Radical manufactured.

 Performance

Top speed	180 mph
0–60 mph	2.7 secs
Power	537 hp
Torque	479 lb-ft

 Engine

Capacity	3.5-liter V6
Type	Twin turbocharged

 Efficiency

Mileage	Not available

 Dimensions

Curb weight	2,492 lb
Power/weight	431 hp/ton
Length	169.3 in

Ariel Atom 3.5

Country of manufacture	United Kingdom		Starting at $49,500

No, they didn't forget to put the bodywork on; the Atom comes like this! The motorcycle-inspired skeletal frame is all about strength (and safety) without weight, and so what if you get wet if it rains? The Atom's figures show how successful the formula is. Ariel's "serious fun" extends to an off-road version called Nomad.

Flip the ignition switch, and the LCD dash springs to life, the shift lights flash, and the fuel pump primes. Press the starter, and the engine instantly fires — ready for track action or city traffic.

 Performance

Top speed	145 mph
0–62 mph	3.1 secs
Power	245 hp
Torque	155 lb-ft

 Engine

Capacity	2.0-liter 4 cylinder
Type	Naturally aspirated

 Efficiency

Mileage	31.4 mpg

 Dimensions

Curb weight	1,367 lb
Power/weight	358 hp/ton
Length	134.3 in

KTM X-Bow R

| Country of manufacture | Austria | Starting at $88,500 |

For almost 10 years, the X-Bow (crossbow) has delighted drivers with its 21st-century take on the simple but effective sports car, as championed by Lotus since the 1950s. Inspired by advanced aerodynamics and carbon-fiber construction from the world of motor racing, it is a usable sports car and track-day weapon.

When launched in 2008, it was the world's first production car with full carbon-composite monocoque. While the underbody is completely flat F1-style, the rear end is a layer cake of foils, flaps, and exposed carbon-fiber tub.

Performance

Top speed	143 mph
0–62 mph	3.9 secs
Power	300 hp
Torque	295 lb-ft

Engine

Capacity	2.0-liter 4 cylinder
Type	Turbocharged

Efficiency

Mileage	34 mpg

Dimensions

Curb weight	1,742 lb
Power/weight	344 hp/ton
Length	147.2 in

Lotus 3-Eleven

Country of manufacture	United Kingdom	Starting at $140,000

Lotus has a reputation for fast road cars and fast racing cars. In the amazing 3-Eleven, it has a car that is fast, and massively capable on road and track. This is the most driver-focused Lotus ever. It follows in the tire tracks of the highly sought-after Lotus 2-Eleven, but updates the formula with more power and fresh design.

The 3-Eleven – with a planned production run of just 311 cars – has gloss-black forged wheels and red AP Racing four-piston calipers. The front splitter, along with rear wing and diffuser, produces 330 pounds of downforce at 150 mph.

 Performance

Top speed	174 mph
0–62 mph	3.4 secs
Power	410 hp
Torque	302 lb-ft

 Engine

Capacity	3.5-liter V6
Type	Supercharged

 **Efficiency**

Mileage	Not available

 **Dimensions**

Curb weight	2,040 lb
Power/weight	402 hp/ton
Length	160.6 in

Caparo T1

Country of manufacture | United Kingdom   Starting at $325,000

Street-legal racing cars come no racier. The T1's power-to-weight ratio is off the scale, due to its light weight and V8 with 583 hp. The result? Mind-bending performance; 5-sec 0–100 mph is claimed. The T1's evolution has been rocky, but it is an astonishing machine from some of the people behind the McLaren F1.

The heart of the T1's powertrain is the all-aluminum 90-degree V8. On standard fuel it claims 583 hp, but put methanol in it, and it puts out 700 hp!

 Performance

Top speed	205 mph
0–62 mph	2.5 secs
Power	583 hp
Torque	310 lb-ft

Engine

Capacity	3.5-liter V8
Type	Naturally aspirated

 Efficiency

Mileage	Not available

 **Dimensions**

Curb weight	1,036 lb
Power/weight	1,125 hp/ton
Length	160.1 in

Elemental RP1

Country of manufacture	United Kingdom	Starting at $128,000

Extreme aerodynamics and light weight are the key to the RP1, the newest road and track car. The doorless two-seater, with a legs-up driving position like that of a Formula 1 car, is the work of mostly ex-McLaren engineers, well versed in making cars go fast. Its targets, like 0–100 mph in 6.4 secs, will surely make it front of the grid.

The hybrid carbon-fiber/aluminum composite tub structure of the RP1, the radical underfloor downforce-generating aerodynamics, and the lightweight chassis make the RP1 a game changer in car design.

 Performance

Top speed	165 mph
0–62 mph	2.8 secs
Power	320 hp
Torque	321 lb-ft

 Engine

Capacity	2.0-liter 4 cylinder
Type	Turbocharged

 Efficiency

Mileage	Not available

 Dimensions

Curb weight	1,270 lb
Power/weight	500 hp/ton
Length	147.2 in

Fast GTs

Gran turismo... just the name conjures up speed, luxury, and sophistication, all the attributes necessary for blasting across continents to exotic locations. GTs can be just as fast and sporty as out-and-out supercars, but with 2+2 cabins and luggage space, are far more accommodating. And they can be just as luxurious as limousines, but with their two-door bodies, look a whole lot more seductive! No wonder some GTs have become the most iconic cars in all of high-performance motoring.

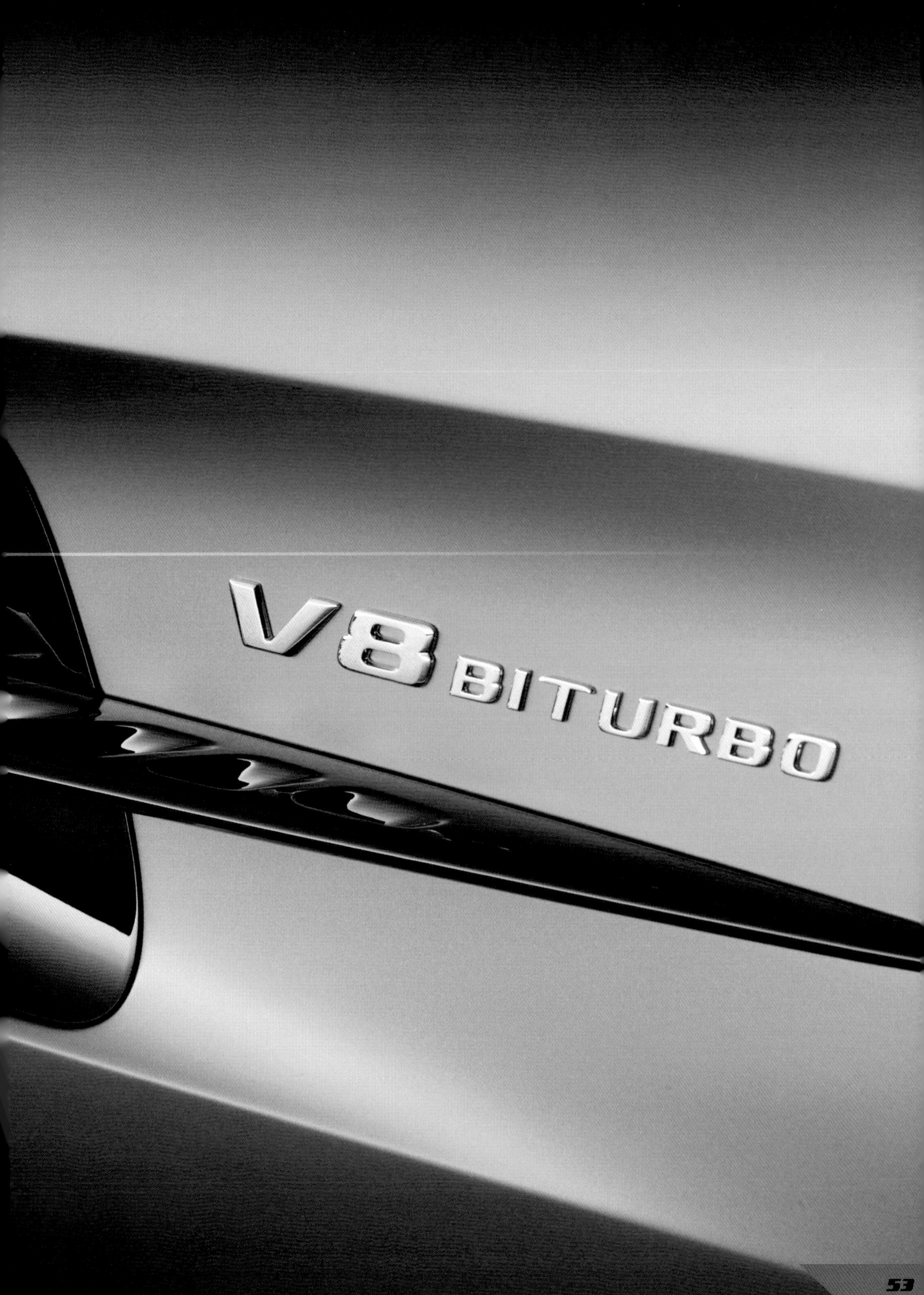
V8 BITURBO

Ferrari 812 Superfast

Country of manufacture	Italy	Starting at $341,712

The classic front-engine, rear-drive Ferrari *gran turismo* is alive and well, and faster than ever. The 812 Superfast is the most powerful and fastest Ferrari in full production. There are no turbos or electric motors, just traditional V12 grunt and 8,500 rpm limit! A "successor" to the Daytona, the Superfast lives up to its name!

The spacious interior, comfortable driving position, and excellent visibility to the front and sides all add to the 812's approachability. And how reassuring is that black prancing horse?

Performance

Top speed	211 mph
0–62 mph	2.9 secs
Power	800 hp
Torque	530 lb-ft

Engine

Capacity	6.5-liter V12
Type	Naturally aspirated

 Efficiency

Mileage	19 mpg

 Dimensions

Curb weight	3,363 lb
Power/weight	476 hp/ton
Length	183.3 in

Rolls-Royce Wraith

Country of manufacture	United Kingdom	Starting at $313,000

Famed for its silence and luxury, the Rolls-Royce is more of a driver's car than ever these days. The V12 engine has always been amply endowed, but now a semi-sporting chassis harnesses the power to surprising effect in the two-door Wraith. In Black Badge form, a dark, moody character meets majestic performance.

The Black Badge Wraith may have been designed for risk takers who laugh in the face of convention, but it's usually revered respect that is aroused when this prize wafts by. Actually, with 0–62 mph in 4.5 secs, "speeds by" would be more accurate.

 Performance

Top speed	155 mph
0–62 mph	4.5 secs
Power	632 hp
Torque	575 lb-ft

 Engine

Capacity	6.6-liter V12
Type	Twin turbocharged

 **Efficiency**

Mileage	19.3 mpg

 **Dimensions**

Curb weight	5,380 lb
Power/weight	235 hp/ton
Length	208.1 in

Lexus LC500h

Country of manufacture	Japan		Starting at $96,5100

This is the car Lexus believe is going to make Porsche drivers think twice! The LC500h is sure to be noticed, with its distinctively different looks and mechanical package. The "h" stands for hybrid – a combination of turbo V6 and electric motor. It's even got two transmissions: a CVT and a regular automatic.

The 500h is a tangle of sharp edges and intersecting lines, but take details like the grille, shallow headlights, front wings that hug the wheels, floating roof, and 3-D-effect rear lights, and there's much to admire.

 Performance

Top speed	155 mph
0–60 mph	4.7 secs
Power	359 hp
Torque	280 lb-ft (gasoline), 221 lb-ft (electric)

 Engine

Capacity	3.5-liter V6
Type	Gasoline/electric hybrid

 **Efficiency**

Mileage	39 mpg

 **Dimensions**

Curb weight	4,436 lb
Power/weight	162 hp/ton
Length	187.4 in

Aston Martin DB11

Country of manufacture	United Kingdom	Starting at $205,000

Aston Martin's new era of cars starts with the DB11. It builds on the power, beauty, and raw charisma of its forebears with new twin-turbo V12 power, clever aerodynamics, and stunning looks. The revolution in its electronics is due to parts sharing with Mercedes. You can even get a DB11 with an AMG V8!

Rear-end lift is reduced by the DB11's AeroBlade, a concealed "virtual" spoiler that is fed by air intakes at the base of each C-pillar. Air is ducted through the bodywork before venting as a jet of air from the aperture in the rear decklid.

 Performance

Top speed	200 mph
0–62 mph	3.9 secs
Power	608 hp
Torque	516 lb-ft

 Engine

Capacity	5.2-liter V12
Type	Twin turbocharged

 **Efficiency**

Mileage	24.8 mpg

 **Dimensions**

Curb weight	3,903 lb
Power/weight	312 hp/ton
Length	186.6 in

Nissan GT-R Nismo

Country of manufacture	Japan	Starting at $175,490

It's "Godzilla" in its most extreme form yet! Japan's distinctively angular 2+2 all-wheel drive coupe has been thrilling drivers on road and track for 10 years now, and it just gets better. Fettled by Nissan tuning arm, Nismo, the best GT-R today boasts 600 hp and acceleration right up there with the world's fastest supercars.

Each Nissan GT-R engine is hand assembled by a single technician (a dash plaque bears his or her signature) in a dust- and temperature-controlled clean room, much like those used for Formula One racing engines. All that for a car you can drive to work in every day!

Performance

Top speed	196 mph
0–60 mph	2.5 secs
Power	600 hp
Torque	481 lb-ft

Engine

Capacity	3.8-liter V6
Type	Twin-turbocharged

 Efficiency

Mileage	23.9 mpg

 Dimensions

Curb weight	3,804 lb
Power/weight	315 hp/ton
Length	184.6 in

Bentley Continental GT Supersports

Country of manufacture	United Kingdom	Starting at $276,000

Bentley's resurgence as part of the VW empire is down to the Continental GT, and with models like the Supersports, its appeal just increases. The W12 engine is in its most-powerful-ever form here, and with a torque vectoring system from the GT3 race car, the all-wheel drive Supersports handles the 710 hp with aplomb.

The Supersports has high-performance carbon-ceramic brakes – the discs are the largest of their type in the world – and a cool carbon-fiber rear spoiler, but do you care when it's all wrapped in diamond-quilted leather and Alcantara luxury?

 Performance

Top speed	209 mph
0–62 mph	3.5 secs
Power	710 hp
Torque	750 lb-ft

 Engine

Capacity	6.0-liter 12 cylinder
Type	Twin turbocharged

 **Efficiency**

Mileage	18.0 mpg

 **Dimensions**

Curb weight	5,027 lb
Power/weight	282 hp/ton
Length	189.2 in

Ford Shelby Mustang GT350R

Country of manufacture	United States	Starting at $69,430

Street legal and track ready, the GT350R is the mightiest Mustang in Ford's history. It is also powered by the most potent naturally aspirated V8 Ford has ever made. Mated to the only transmission choice – a six-speed manual – the pony car gets to 60 mph in under four seconds, and the V8 revs to 8,250 rpm. Yee-haw!

At 102 hp per liter, the V8 is Ford's most powerful naturally aspirated road car engine … ever. With R version's light weight – no rear seats and carbon-fiber wheels – acceleration is fierce.

Performance

Top speed	190 mph
0–60 mph	3.9 secs
Power	533 hp
Torque	526 lb-ft

Engine

Capacity	5.2-liter V8
Type	Naturally aspirated

Efficiency

Mileage	14–21 mpg

 Dimensions

Curb weight	3,656 lb
Power/weight	292 hp/ton
Length	188.3

BMW M4 CS

Country of manufacture	Germany	Starting at $105,700

M cars are always special – and fast. But they are not always fast enough for everyone, which is why BMW makes special-edition M cars. The breed began with the M3 Evolution in the 1980s, and its successor is the M4 CS: lighter, more aerodynamic, and more powerful – and able to lap the Nürburgring in 7 minutes 38 seconds.

Borrowing performance parts from the M4 GTS and the CLS, the CS (Club Sport) uses carbon fiber-reinforced plastic for hood, roof, rear diffuser, and driveshaft. BMW has even thrown out molded door handles and gotten natty with fabric door pulls!

Performance

Top speed	174 mph
0–62 mph	3.9 secs
Power	460 hp
Torque	442 lb-ft

Engine

Capacity	3.0-liter straight 6
Type	Twin turbocharged

Efficiency

Mileage	34 mpg

Dimensions

Curb weight	3,484 lb
Power/weight	264 hp/ton
Length	183.9 in

Chevrolet Camaro ZL1

Country of manufacture	United States		Starting at $64,195

Chevrolet was so confident of its new ZL1 it took it to the Nürburgring for a few hot laps – with a very respectable 7 minutes 16 seconds result. The American muscle car icon's supercharged 650 hp V8 can be had with a six-speed manual or 10-speed automatic. The latest model has lost weight and gained bigger Brembo brakes.

New aero features include a carbon-fiber rear wing, while air deflectors and dive planes on the front fascia produce grip-generating downforce to help the car stick harder and drive faster in the turns.

 Performance

Top speed	198 mph
0–60 mph	3.5 secs
Power	650 hp
Torque	650 lb-ft

 Engine

Capacity	6.2-liter V8
Type	Supercharged

 Efficiency

Mileage	16–20 mpg

 Dimensions

Curb weight	3,934 lb
Power/weight	330 hp/ton
Length	188.3 in

Mercedes-AMG GT R

Country of manufacture	Germany		Starting at $157,000

Racing improves the breed, and for proof look no further than Mercedes' fastest coupe. The GT R is the most motorsport-influenced car they have ever made. GT3 influences extend to carbon body parts, Race Mode suspension setting, active rear steering, 585 hp, and even Nürburgring "Green Hell" paint color!

The GT R's Panamericana grille – as once used on AMG road racers of old – has 15 vertical struts. On the GT R's rear, over the badge, sits a large, static airfoil.

Performance

Top speed	198 mph
0–62 mph	3.6 secs
Power	585 hp
Torque	516 lb-ft

Engine

Capacity	4-liter V8
Type	Twin turbocharged

 Efficiency

Mileage	24.8 mpg

 Dimensions

Curb weight	3,594 lb
Power/weight	326 hp/ton
Length	179.2 in

Porsche 911 Turbo S

Country of manufacture	Germany	Starting at $190,700

Most cars are turbocharged these days, but there's still only one Turbo: the 911 in its ultimate road specification. The wide-body 911 shape is familiar, but under the rear lid is almost 600 hp of turbocharged flat six, powering all four wheels for fantastic acceleration when you want it, and refined cruising when you don't.

The interior, like the smooth coupe body shape, still has plenty in common with the first 911 of 1963 – like the big rev counter behind the steering wheel. But in Turbo S form, it's got a lot more power!

 Performance

Top speed	205 mph
0–62 mph	2.9 secs
Power	580 hp
Torque	553 lb-ft

 Engine

Capacity	3.8-liter flat 6
Type	Twin turbocharged

 Efficiency

Mileage	31 mpg

 Dimensions

Curb weight	3,693 lb
Power/weight	314 hp/ton
Length	177.4 in

Maserati GranTurismo MC Stradale

Country of manufacture | **Italy**   **Starting at $144,000**

Classic name, classic looks, and with its old-school, naturally aspirated 4.7-liter V8, classic engineering too – with the booming engine soundtrack to prove it! Though 10 years old now, the beautiful GranTurismo in its lightest and most powerful MC Stradale form is as evocative as fast Italian coupes come.

 Performance

Top speed	188 mph
0–62 mph	4.5 secs
Power	460 hp
Torque	383 lb-ft

Engine

Capacity	4.7-liter V8
Type	Naturally aspirated

Efficiency

Mileage	19.6 mpg

Dimensions

Curb weight	3,969 lb
Power/weight	232 hp/ton
Length	194.2 in

In the original MC Stradale – the racing version used in the Maserati Trofeo Championship – the back seats were ditched to save weight and make it go faster. In the later model, there's luxury for four passengers.

Sporting Sedans and Wagons

▶ Meet the luxury sedans and wagons that think they are sports cars! There is certainly nothing tame about these four-door sedans – and one five-door wagon – when it comes to power and rocket ship acceleration. Some have their top speeds limited to 155 mph, but others max out at 190, or even 200 mph! And whether a gas-guzzling V12 or clean, battery powered, all have one thing in common: plenty of room for the whole family.

Audi RS6 quattro

Country of manufacture	Germany		Starting at $106,000

Audi defined the high-performance wagon with the RS2 of 1994, and the marque's four rings have been synonymous with the breed ever since. The latest RS6 is the ultimate all-wheel drive, all roads, all seasons, everyday performance car. If the speed limiter is taken off, it'll do almost 190 mph.

An automotive writer described the RS6's interior as being "built from granite made to look like plastic." The interior gets a high-performance makeover, but is still fully functioning as a spacious and practical station wagon.

 Performance

Top speed	155 mph
0–62 mph	3.7 secs
Power	605 hp
Torque	553 lb-ft

 Engine

Capacity	4.0-liter V8
Type	Twin turbocharged

 **Efficiency**

Mileage	29.4 mpg

 **Dimensions**

Curb weight	4,300 lb
Power/weight	281 hp/ton
Length	196 in

Jaguar XE SV Project 8

Country of manufacture	United Kingdom	Starting at $195,000

Meet the most powerful road-going Jag of all time. The XE started life as a mild-mannered four-door, but after a visit to Jaguar's Special Vehicle Operations, emerged as a fire-breathing monster. Its supercar performance is thanks to a supercharged V8 with 600 hp. The Track Pack version ditches the back seats to save weight.

Jaguar are making only 300 Project 8s – all left-hand drive – so they will be collector's items. While everything is dedicated to optimum performance, including F1-style silicon nitride ceramic wheel bearings, the cabin comforts have not been forgotten.

 Performance

Top speed	200 mph
0–62 mph	3.7 secs
Power	600 hp
Torque	516 lb-ft

 Engine

Capacity	5.0-liter V8
Type	Supercharged

 **Efficiency**

Mileage	Not available

 **Dimensions**

Curb weight	3,848 lb
Power/weight	312 hp/ton
Length	185.6 in

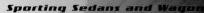

BMW M760Li V12

Country of manufacture	Germany		Starting at $180,000

No four-door sedan over sixteen feet long and 2.4 tons should be able to get from 0–62 mph in under four seconds. But the M760Li can, and it is the German firm's flagship – a car in with a chance of being the world's greatest sporting limousine. It comes with Launch Control – so don't take it on in the stoplight grand prix!

Perhaps the most techie car in its class – there's a gesture control to change infotainment choice or volume, seats that massage you, and a key with a touchscreen that will tell you fuel level and switch on preset heating. James Bond's Q would love it!

Performance

Top speed	155 mph
0–62 mph	3.7 secs
Power	609 hp
Torque	590 lb-ft

Engine

Capacity	6.6-liter V12
Type	Twin turbocharged

 Efficiency

Mileage	22.1 mpg

 Dimensions

Curb weight	4,972 lb
Power/weight	245 hp/ton
Length	206.6 in

Cadillac CTS-V

Country of manufacture	United States		Starting at $87,990

The supercharged 6.2-liter V8 is performance currency in North America, but few cars use it as well as the CTS-V – four initials that sum up the very essence of "super sedan." The automatic rear-wheel drive car can blast to 200 mph, but with its sports suspension, it's far more than a drag race special. It corners like a racer too!

The Carbon Black Package CTS-V has the power to stop, as well as the power to go. Brakes are huge Brembo discs; six-piston at the rear. The wheels are huge too.

Performance

Top speed	200 mph
0–60 mph	3.6 secs
Power	640 hp
Torque	630 lb-ft

Engine

Capacity	6.2-liter V8
Type	Supercharged

 Efficiency

Mileage	14–20 mpg

 Dimensions

Curb weight	4,141 lb
Power/weight	309 hp/ton
Length	195.5 in

Mercedes-AMG S65L

Country of manufacture	Germany	Starting at $229,500

This Merc S-Class with the works goes by the name of AMG S65. To the awesome luxury and technology already in the world's favorite limo, AMG adds a sporting makeover including a twin-turbo V12 engine and close to 750 lb-ft of torque. Performance is totally effortless – and it's all as smooth and quiet as any S-Class!

The interior of the S65L is lit by about 300 LEDs – there's not a normal light bulb anywhere! There are seven color options and various lighting zones to dial up a lighting plan to suit your mood and needs.

 Performance

Top speed	155 mph
0–62 mph	4.3 secs
Power	630 hp
Torque	738 lb-ft

 Engine

Capacity	6.0-liter V12
Type	Twin turbocharged

 Efficiency

Mileage	23.7 mpg

 Dimensions

Curb weight	4,961 lb
Power/weight	254 hp/ton
Length	208.1 in

Bentley Flying Spur W12 S

Country of manufacture	United Kingdom	Starting at $201,500

Bentley has been making fast cars since the 1920s, *and* winning Le Mans with them. But this ultimate Flying Spur takes things further – by being the first four-door Bentley to break the 200-mph barrier. Outside, there are 21-inch wheels and carbon-ceramic brakes to make sure it slows down as fast as it accelerates!

The winged B says you have arrived, and in the W12 S you most probably got there fast! But for gentle exploring, you might enjoy options like the veneered picnic tables with vanity mirrors, bottle cooler, and champagne flutes.

 Performance

Top speed	202 mph
0–62 mph	4.5 secs
Power	635 hp
Torque	605 lb-ft

Engine

Capacity	6.0-liter W12
Type	Twin turbocharged

 Efficiency

Mileage	19.8 mpg

 Dimensions

Curb weight	5,457 lb
Power/weight	233 hp/ton
Length	208.6 in

Alfa Romeo Giulia 2.9 Quadrifoglio

Country of manufacture	Italy	Starting at $73,700

At last, the famous Alfa Romeo badge is back on a performance sedan that really means business. The Quadrifoglio (it means four-leaf clover) gets 510 hp and is pace scintillating enough to take on powerful German rivals. But it's also an Alfa, so it looks great, sounds great, and has a distinct Italian character. *Ciao bella!*

The Alfa badge dates from 1910 when Alfa (Anonima Lombarda Fabbrica Automobili) started. The red cross represents Milan, which is Alfa's hometown. The snake spitting out a human stands for change and rebirth. Now you know!

 Performance

Top speed	191 mph
0–62 mph	3.9 secs
Power	510 hp
Torque	442 lb-ft

 Engine

Capacity	2.9-liter V6
Type	Twin turbocharged

 **Efficiency**

Mileage	34.4 mpg

 **Dimensions**

Curb weight	3,360 lb
Power/weight	304 hp/ton
Length	182.6 in

Tesla Model S P100D "Ludicrous"

Country of manufacture	United States	Starting at $175,500

It's big, luxurious, all electric, and ludicrously fast, as the name of its sports driving mode attests. Top speed is pegged back to 155 mph, but on initial acceleration it's as fast as Porsche's fastest sports car. The two-motor top version Model S is in the record books for its speed, and will do over 300 miles on a charge.

The Model S is the world's top-selling electric car, and who wouldn't want a car with a Ludicrous mode? It refers to the speed at which this car accelerates – not too shabby for a big luxury five-seater!

Performance

Top speed	155 mph
0–60 mph	2.7 secs
Power	603 hp
Torque	713 lb-ft

Engine

Capacity	100 kWh
Type	Plug-in electric

Efficiency

Mileage	Not available

Dimensions

Curb weight	4,648 lb
Power/weight	259 hp/ton
Length	196 in

Aston Martin Rapide S

Country of manufacture	United Kingdom		Starting at $194,500

If James Bond ever needs a family car here it is: Aston Martin's first four-door since the 1980s Lagonda. A stretched version of the superseded DB9, the Rapide looks, sounds, and drives like an Aston Martin sports car, but with extra doors and rear seat room. Its V12 is pure Aston, but the future Rapide E model will be all electric!

To start the V12 in the Rapide you have to insert a large glass key in a slot on the dashboard. The engine sounds just as good as an Aston sports car – and this four-seater is almost as fast!

Performance

Top speed	203 mph
0–62 mph	4.4 secs
Power	560 hp
Torque	465 lb-ft

Engine

Capacity	6.0-liter V12
Type	Naturally aspirated

Efficiency

Mileage	21.9 mpg

Dimensions

Curb weight	4,388 lb
Power/weight	255 hp/ton
Length	197.6 in

Porsche Panamera Turbo S E-Hybrid

Country of manufacture	Germany	Starting at $186,200

Five-door wagons don't come with any more impressive numbers than this plug-in gas/electric Porsche. How does 97 mpg and 0–125 mph in just 11.7 secs sound? Plus, there's room for four people and the dog! The secret is a combination of V8 and electric motor. It's mean, and green, and very, very keen.

Porsche has banned most of the buttons in the latest Panamera; now it's all touchscreen (12-in in the dash) and voice control. Very high-tech – just like the car's hybrid drivetrain.

Performance

Top speed	193 mph
0–62 mph	3.4 secs
Power	680 hp
Torque	627 lb-ft

Engine

Capacity	4.0-liter V8
Type	Gasoline/electric hybrid

Efficiency

Mileage	97 mpg

 Dimensions

Curb weight	5,259 lb
Power/weight	259 hp/ton
Length	198.8 in

Volvo S60 Polestar

Country of manufacture	Sweden	Starting at $73,500

Polestar knows a lot about making safety-first Swedes get a move on: it has been racing Volvos for years. Now it's heating-up Volvos you can buy, and the S60 (and V60 wagon) is its best yet – swift, rewarding, safe, and efficient. Get it while you can: Polestar's future lies in an all-new range of high-performance electric cars.

Volvos can be fast, and satisfying too, and none better than a Volvo that's had a makeover from Polestar. They are used to racing Volvos, so know everything there is about making an S60 go fast!

Performance

Top speed	155 mph
0–62 mph	4.7 secs
Power	367 hp
Torque	347 lb-ft

Engine

Capacity	2.0-liter 4 cylinder
Type	Turbocharged and supercharged

Efficiency

Mileage	29 mpg

 Dimensions

Curb weight	3,894 lb
Power/weight	188 hp/ton
Length	182.5 in

Dodge SRT Hellcat Charger

Country of manufacture	United States		Starting at $67,995

Claiming the title of world's most powerful production sedan, the Hellcat version of the four-door Charger has a massive 707 horses to propel it, enough even to keep its Cadillac CTS-V rival honest. In the two-door Challenger version you get 840 hp, and the fastest quarter-mile of any production car ever.

 Performance

Top speed	204 mph
0–60 mph	3.7 secs
Power	707 hp
Torque	650 lb-ft

Engine

Capacity	6.2-liter V8
Type	Supercharged

Efficiency

Mileage	13–22 mpg

This family performance sedan with its sinister looks comes to a halt using the largest brakes ever offered in a Chrysler Group vehicle – 15.4-inch Brembo two-piece rotors with six-piston calipers.

Dimensions

Curb weight	4,575 lb
Power/weight	309 hp/ton
Length	200.8 in

Maserati Quattroporte GTS

Country of manufacture	Italy	Starting at $151,000

The Maserati Four-Door – the name definitely sounds better in Italian – was the fastest four-door sedan in the world in the mid-1960s. In fact, it was pretty much the only one, Maserati being first to combine a racing engine with a big sedan body. Now in its sixth generation, it comes with a Ferrari-derived V8 engine.

The cabin is swathed in the finest leather, the headrests are embossed with the Trident logo, and there's plenty of room on sumptuous seats front and back. This Italian beauty comes with all the latest mod cons.

 Performance

Top speed	191 mph
0–62 mph	4.7 secs
Power	530 hp
Torque	524 lb-ft

 Engine

Capacity	3.8-liter V8
Type	Twin turbocharged

 **Efficiency**

Mileage	26.4 mpg

 **Dimensions**

Curb weight	4,190 lb
Power/weight	253 hp/ton
Length	207.2 in

Holden Commodore HSV GTSR W1

Country of manufacture | **Australia** | **Starting at $123,000**

Say hello – and goodbye – to the greatest Aussie V8 muscle car ever...and also the last. It's GM Holden's most ferocious beast yet, in a long line of high-performance Commodores. This "thunder from down under" in ultimate W1 version is a collector's edition.

The hot Aussie Commodore, along with all local production, ended in 2017, but it bowed out in style with the W1 edition: this rear wing is all most people will ever see of it!

Performance

Top speed	155 mph
0–62 mph	4.2 secs
Power	644 hp
Torque	601 lb-ft

Engine

Capacity	6.2-liter V8
Type	Supercharged

 Efficiency

Mileage	17.1 mpg

 Dimensions

Curb weight	4,178 lb
Power/weight	308 hp/ton
Length	198.6 in

Convertibles

▶ Convertible, cabriolet, soft-top, ragtop, spider (and sometimes spyder) – whatever name you call them, cars without roofs open up a whole new world of high-performance motoring. With the wind in your hair and the roar of the exhaust ringing in your ears, convertibles offer high-octane, high-profile thrills – especially when they are as fast as these beauties...

Jaguar F-Type SVR

Country of manufacture | **United Kingdom** | **Starting at $153,500**

Like its spiritual forebear, the E-Type, the F-Type comes in both coupe and cabriolet forms. Either car is quick in top of the range 575 hp SVR form, but opt for the convertible, and top speed drops from the magic 200 mph to a mere 195! That's still a great deal faster than any E-Type. In fact, it's the fastest Jag since the mighty XJ220.

The cat's aerodynamics include a carbon-fiber active rear wing and rear venturi to reduce lift and drag. And the bonus with the roof off: the uncensored soundtrack of V8 burbles from the titanium pipes, with lots of pops and bangs when you change gear!

Performance

Top speed	195 mph
0–62 mph	3.7 secs
Power	575 hp
Torque	516 lb-ft

Engine

Capacity	5.0-liter V8
Type	Supercharged

Efficiency

Mileage	25.0 mpg

Dimensions

Curb weight	3,793 lb
Power/weight	303 hp/ton
Length	176.2 in

Alfa Romeo 4C Spider

Country of manufacture	Italy	Starting at $66,900

The 4C does what Alfas have always done best: go fast, look great, and handle beautifully. The key to its scintillating pace is light weight and a giant turbocharger, which together make its small 1.7-liter engine feel (and sound!) like more of a grunter than its 240 hp would suggest. With 0–62 mph in 4.5 secs, it's a visceral experience.

The much-disliked ugly bug-eye lights that marred the front of the earlier model have been replaced with traditional headlights. Now that that is sorted out, pundits can talk about just how beautiful this Alfa really is.

 Performance

Top speed	160 mph
0–62 mph	4.5 secs
Power	240 hp
Torque	258 lb-ft

 Engine

Capacity	1.7-liter 4 cylinder
Type	Turbocharged

☑ **Efficiency**

Mileage	40.9 mpg

 **Dimensions**

Curb weight	2203 lb
Power/weight	218 hp/ton
Length	157.1 in

BMW M240i

Country of manufacture	Germany	Starting at $48,800

There's no M2 convertible (yet), but there is the M240i cabriolet – and it's almost as good! Small, agile and immensely chuckable, there's nothing not to like in this 340-hp baby bombshell that can sprint from rest to 62 mph in just five seconds. Plus, there are seats in the back, so you get to share the thrills with friends.

If the M240i's performance doesn't make you app-y, its user-friendly connectivity will. All your favorite apps appear on the new-look dashboard.

Performance

Top speed	155 mph
0–62 mph	5.0 secs
Power	340 hp
Torque	369 lb-ft

Engine

Capacity	3.0-liter straight 6
Type	Turbocharged

Efficiency

Mileage	34 mpg

Dimensions

Curb weight	3,726 lb
Power/weight	182 hp/ton
Length	175.4 in

Aston Martin V12 Vantage

Country of manufacture | **United Kingdom**   **Starting at $200,500**

Vantage is a famous Aston Martin name, reserved for its fastest cars, and this specimen doesn't disappoint. It might be Aston's oldest model (dating to 2005), but with 0–62 mph in 3.9 seconds, it's as fast as the 2017 DB11! Originally a V8 coupe, the top spec today is the hand-built convertible body with V12 under the hood.

Aston's un-turbocharged V12 is old-school and all the better for it: it is one of the best-sounding engines in production. This car has pure charisma, along with storming performance.

 Performance

Top speed	201 mph
0–62 mph	3.9 secs
Power	573 hp
Torque	457 lb-ft

Engine

Capacity	6.0-liter V12
Type	Naturally aspirated

 Efficiency

Mileage	19.2 mpg

 **Dimensions**

Curb weight	3,671 lb
Power/weight	312 hp/ton
Length	172.6 in

Mazda MX-5

Country of manufacture	Japan	Starting at $24,500

The world's favorite sports car was a hit the day it arrived in 1989, and four model-generations later, it's still as popular. The MX-5 has never been the most powerful or fastest car in the world, but it has always been one of the most fun to drive, doing really well those things that old British sports cars did badly!

The designers/engineers at Mazda are all about *Jinba Ittai*, which is the unity of car and driver – yes, even when it comes to having somewhere to put your coffee! But car/driver unity shows up most of all in how sweet the MX-5 is to drive.

Performance

Top speed	133 mph
0–62 mph	7.3 secs
Power	160 hp
Torque	147 lb-ft

Engine

Capacity	2.0-liter 4 cylinder
Type	Naturally aspirated

Efficiency

Mileage	47.1 mpg

 Dimensions

Curb weight	2,370 lb
Power/weight	135 hp/ton
Length	154.1 in

Fiat Abarth 124

The Fiat 124 Spider was one of the most popular 1960s sports cars. Now it's back, and in Abarth form! It shares vehicle architecture with the Mazda MX-5, but that hasn't stopped the Italians making it look supercool, with its thrusting nose (like the Pininfarina original), hood power bulges and racy paint job.

This car's controls shout *guida sportiva* (sporty drive) in true Italian tradition. The small diameter steering wheel (with red center mark), big rev counter, grippy seats, and well-spaced pedals all say: drive me!

 Performance

Top speed	144 mph
0–62 mph	6.8 secs
Power	170 hp
Torque	184 lb-ft

 Engine

Capacity	1.4-liter 4 cylinder
Type	Turbocharged

 **Efficiency**

Mileage	44.1 mpg

 **Dimensions**

Curb weight	2,337 lb
Power/weight	145 hp/ton
Length	159.6 in

Porsche 718 Boxster S

Country of manufacture	Germany	Starting at $72,000

It's wind-in-the-hair thrills with the 177-mph, mid-engined, two-seat Boxster in sporty S form. The "718" in its badge revives the name of an old Porsche racing car. Like all Boxsters it has a "boxer" engine, with horizontally opposed cylinders, but since 2016 it's a four-cylinder turbo – even Porsches must downsize!

The Boxster has always had a generous rear end (there's an engine under that flat rear deck), but in latest 718 form it looks sharper. In the corners, the handling is sharp too!

Performance

Top speed	177 mph
0–62 mph	4.6 secs
Power	350 hp
Torque	310 lb-ft

Engine

Capacity	2.5-liter flat 4
Type	Turbocharged

 Efficiency

Mileage	34.9 mpg

 Dimensions

Curb weight	3,153 lb
Power/weight	222 hp/ton
Length	172.4 in

Mercedes-AMG SL65

| **Starting at $222,000**

The Mercedes SL has an honorable history on road and track. Today, SL is a byword for the most high-tech and civilized convertible motoring on the planet. But in AMG SL65 form, that doesn't mean slow. This monster SL's top speed is limited, but 0–62 mph in 4.0 secs shows this mighty Merc's true performance colors.

Not only does this glam Merc have 12 cylinders, its Bang & Olufsen audio system blasts out 900 watts of power through 12 speakers. All the better for you and anyone in a three-mile radius to hear.

 Performance

Top speed	155 mph
0–62 mph	4.0 secs
Power	630 hp
Torque	738 lb-ft

 Engine

Capacity	6.0-liter V12
Type	Twin turbocharged

 **Efficiency**

Mileage	23.7 mpg

 **Dimensions**

Curb weight	4,300 lb
Power/weight	293 hp/ton
Length	182.3 in

Morgan Aero 8

Country of manufacture	United Kingdom	Starting at $165,000

With its old-school looks, it could only be that unique phenomenon that is a Morgan motor car. But as well as being 170 mph fast, this is a very modern Morgan – there's no wooden body frame, and under the long hood is a BMW 4.8-liter V8. With the top down and the exhaust booming, country cruising was never better!

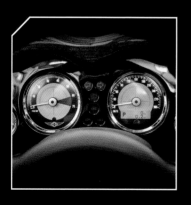

It's a Morgan, so what else but a wood dashboard and big dials? But in the Aero 8, tradition goes hand in hand with high-tech, as well as a great deal of power courtesy of that BMW V8.

 Performance

Top speed	170 mph
0–62 mph	4.5 secs
Power	367 hp
Torque	361 lb-ft

 Engine

Capacity	4.8-liter V8
Type	Naturally aspirated

Efficiency

Mileage	23.3 mpg

 Dimensions

Curb weight	2,602 lb
Power/weight	282 hp/ton
Length	163.3 in

Lamborghini Huracan LP610-4

Country of manufacture	Italy		Starting at $235,000

Lamborghini invented the supercar 50 years ago with the Miura, and as the Huracan shows, they've not lost their touch. It's the epitome of contemporary cool. The Spyder version of the 200-mph LP610-4 (610 is hp, 4 for all-wheel drive) is the best way of hearing a naturally aspirated V10 screaming to 8,250 rpm!

Top down, V10 burbling, this is surely the only way to arrive on the Italian Riviera! With a cockpit like this, the drive there would be pure unbridled pleasure.

 Performance

Top speed	201 mph
0–62 mph	3.4 secs
Power	610 hp
Torque	413 lb-ft

 Engine

Capacity	5.2-liter V10
Type	Naturally aspirated

 **Efficiency**

Mileage	22.6 mpg

 **Dimensions**

Curb weight	3,131 lb
Power/weight	390 hp/ton
Length	175.6 in

Chevrolet Corvette Z07

Country of manufacture	United States		Starting at $96,757

The legend of America's only true sports car continues! Any of the new (seventh-generation) Corvette family, which resurrected the Stingray name, is a powerhouse of performance and styling. But in 6.2-liter supercharged Z06 form – and ideally fitted with the Z07 Performance Pack – it's a world-class contender.

The Z07 package adds adjustable aero components, like the front winglets for convincing downforce, Michelin Pilot Super Sport Cup tires for top grip, and Brembo carbon-ceramic brake rotors.

 Performance

Top speed	205 mph
0–60 mph	2.9 secs
Power	650 hp
Torque	650 lb-ft

 Engine

Capacity	6.2-liter V8
Type	Supercharged

 **Efficiency**

Mileage	15–22 mpg

 **Dimensions**

Curb weight	3,524 lb
Power/weight	369 hp/ton
Length	177.9 in

Lotus Elise Cup 250

Country of manufacture	United Kingdom		Starting at $60,500

The Elise has been delighting racers for years, and with each new version it gets a little lighter, a little more powerful, and a whole lot more fun to drive. This new Cup 250 is the fastest Elise to date. Its supercharged 1.8-liter engine delivers 243 hp that lets it sprint to 62 mph from a standstill in sub four seconds!

The latest version of the Elise Cup 250 is a lightweight in every respect – except its performance. The engineers in Norfolk, UK, have "added lightness" by using carbon fiber, titanium and aluminum. And if it isn't needed, it isn't on the car!

 Performance

Top speed	154 mph
0–62 mph	3.9 secs
Power	243 hp
Torque	184 lb-ft

 Engine

Capacity	1.8-liter 4 cylinder
Type	Supercharged

 **Efficiency**

Mileage	37.7 mpg

 **Dimensions**

Curb weight	2,053 lb
Power/weight	237 hp/ton
Length	150.6 in

Supercars

▶ Impossibly low, sleek, and fast looking even when standing still, supercars are the poster stars of the motoring world. Photographs of them in exotic locations have adorned bedroom walls for generations, ever since the blueprint for the first modern supercars was established in the 1960s. Today, there's more choice than ever from more supercar companies than ever, all using a vast array of new technologies. But some things never change: they are faster than ever, but still

ENGINE OIL FILL
SAE 0W - 40
SYNTHETIC ENGINE OIL
RECOMMENDED

Honda/Acura NSX

Country of manufacture	United States		Starting at $156,000

The sleek NSX is a technological tour de force from the makers of the Civic hatchback! With a V6, three electric motors, and all-wheel drive, it's fast and sure-footed, but easy to drive. The first NSX (1991) remade the supercar as something you could use every day, a tradition the new model takes into the supercar stratosphere.

Interwoven under the leather dash panel is the exposed mid-frame – a functioning chassis member like those on a naked sport bike. An ultra-thin A-pillar and low-mounted instrument panel maximize the driver's view of the road.

 Performance

Top speed	191 mph
0–62 mph	3.3 secs
Power	581 hp
Torque	476 lb-ft

 Engine

Capacity	3.5-liter V6
Type	Gasoline/electric hybrid

 Efficiency

Mileage	28.2 mpg

 **Dimensions**

Curb weight	3,916 lb
Power/weight	297 hp/ton
Length	176.7 in

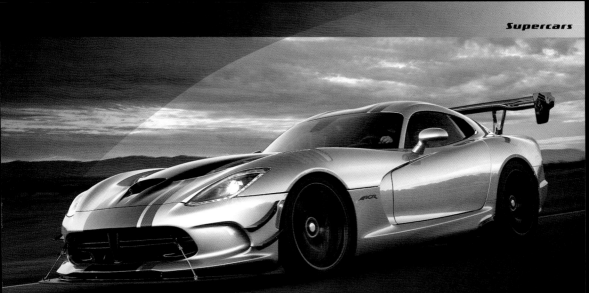

Dodge Viper

Country of manufacture	United States		Starting at $76,500

The all-American Viper is the supercar they couldn't kill! The V10-powered two-seater has been around in one form or another since 1992, but people just love it so much, newer ones are still hot. And the Viper of 2017 – sadly, its final year – is doubly hot. It bowed out in style: faster, louder, and more brash than ever.

Over eight liters of V10 engine is not for the fainthearted! Watch those revs or this Viper will bite – one reason the latest (and last) version comes with electronic stability control.

Performance

Top speed	206 mph
0–62 mph	3.4 secs
Power	645 hp
Torque	600 lb-ft

Engine

Capacity	8.4-liter V10
Type	Naturally aspirated

Efficiency

Mileage	12–19 mpg

Dimensions

Curb weight	3,378 lb
Power/weight	382 hp/ton
Length	175.7 in

BMW i8

Country of manufacture	Germany	Starting at $147,500

Way ahead of its time when launched, the i8 is a plug-in hybrid with a tiny three-cylinder engine at the back and a big electric motor up front, with batteries under the cabin floor. Its looks are as progressive as the technology, and its figures astonishing: 0–62 mph in 4.4 secs, 134 mpg, and up to 75 mph on electric alone.

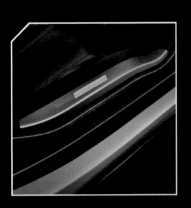

In the special-edition Frozen Yellow i8, the door-sill finisher declares its exclusive status, and in the cabin, the seats have yellow stitching, and the headrests are embossed with the i8 logo. This car's so good, you'll never let it go!

 Performance

Top speed	155 mph
0–62 mph	4.4 secs
Power	362 hp
Torque	420 lb-ft

 Engine

Capacity	1.5-liter 3 cylinder
Type	Gasoline/electric hybrid

 Efficiency

Mileage	134.5 mpg

 Dimensions

Curb weight	3,440 lb
Power/weight	210 hp/ton
Length	184.6 in

Ford GT

Country of manufacture	Canada	Starting at $450,000

The fastest-ever Ford is a thinly disguised racing car for the road, in that it is just like its ancestor, the iconic 1960s GT40. It has even followed in the GT40's tire tracks by winning at Le Mans. A true Ferrari/McLaren rival, the GT boasts massive power from the turbocharged V6, an incredible top speed, and stunning looks.

Only 500 Ford GTs were made, and they all sold. But if you had one, this is what you would see on its 10-in digital display when the GT hit its top speed of 216 mph.

 ## Performance

Top speed	216 mph
0–62 mph	2.9 secs (estimate)
Power	655 hp
Torque	550 lb-ft

 ## Engine

Capacity	3.5-liter V6
Type	Twin turbocharged

 ## Efficiency

Mileage	16.8 mpg

 ## Dimensions

Curb weight	3,054 lb
Power/weight	429 hp/ton
Length	187.5 in

Lamborghini Aventador S

Country of manufacture	Italy	Starting at $409,500

No one does ferocious speed and outlandish looks better than Lamborghini. And the Aventador in 740 hp S form is a poster car in the mold of greats like the Countach. Named after a fighting bull, the flagship supercar's V12 is mounted behind the seats. Power? 740 hp! And it's not even turbocharged!

Center stacks don't come much wider than this. It's a real button fest! Black trim and yellow piping are very Lambo, as is the rev counter dominating the instrument binnacle.

 Performance

Top speed	217 mph
0–62 mph	2.9 secs
Power	740 hp
Torque	509 lb-ft

 Engine

Capacity	6.5-liter V12
Type	Naturally aspirated

 **Efficiency**

Mileage	16.7 mpg

 **Dimensions**

Curb weight	3,473 lb
Power/weight	426 hp/ton
Length	188.9 in

Porsche 911 GT2 RS

Country of manufacture	Germany	Starting at $294,250

It's the ultimate 911! Never before has Porsche's iconic sports car been this powerful and driver focused. It debuted at the Goodwood Festival of Speed in 2017, and speed is this car's middle name. It is two-wheel drive but has four-wheel steering for extra agility, and there's a Weissach handling pack option for really serious drivers.

Not fast enough for you? You need the Weissach pack. It replaces key components – like the roof – with carbon fiber to save weight. You can even get a roll cage made of…titanium!

Performance

Top speed	211 mph
0–62 mph	2.8 secs
Power	700 hp
Torque	553 lb-ft

Engine

Capacity	3.8-liter flat 6
Type	Twin turbocharged

 Efficiency

Mileage	24 mpg

 Dimensions

Curb weight	3,241 lb
Power/weight	432 hp/ton
Length	178.9 in

Audi R8 V10 Plus

Country of manufacture	Germany	Starting at $175,000

Supercars don't come more user-friendly than the R8 – here's a 205-mph car your grandparents could drive! That doesn't mean it is boring. Audi has avoided turbocharging its V10, with the result that it is powerful and revs to past 8,000 rpm, but sounds majestic. There's a special button to push to make the exhaust sound even louder!

Twenty-four R8 V10 Plus "selection 24h" models will be built, combining competition-inspired styling enhancements, including a sport exhaust for further amplification of the R8's much-loved 10-cylinder soundtrack.

 Performance

Top speed	205 mph
0–62 mph	3.2 secs
Power	610 hp
Torque	413 lb-ft

 Engine

Capacity	5.2-liter V10
Type	Naturally aspirated

 **Efficiency**

Mileage	23.0 mpg

 **Dimensions**

Curb weight	3,429 lb
Power/weight	356 hp/ton
Length	174.3 in

Spyker C8 Preliator

Country of manufacture	United Kingdom	Starting at $429,000

Preliator – it means warrior – is everything a Spyker should be: advanced, individual, and inspired by airplanes. Spyker is a Dutch brand with an aviation heritage, known since 2000 as a supercar manufacturer. The latest C8 Preliator has a mighty Koenigsegg engine! It is one of few 600-hp cars with a manual gearbox.

Much of the C8's design is heavily inspired by Spyker's aviation heritage, but the Latin motto pressed into the exhaust is very down-to-earth: for the tenacious, no road is impassable.

 Performance

Top speed	201 mph
0–62 mph	3.6 secs
Power	600 hp
Torque	442 lb-ft

 Engine

Capacity	5.0-liter V8
Type	Naturally aspirated

 Efficiency

Mileage	Not available

 Dimensions

Curb weight	3,065 lb
Power/weight	392 hp/ton
Length	182.2 in

McLaren 720S

Country of manufacture	United Kingdom		Starting at $283,500

Britain's supercar success gets better and better. And the cars keep getting faster! New for 2017, the 720S was the first of a new range of Super Series cars that began with the 2011 12C. It is a break from what came before, including its design and aerodynamics, said to offer twice the downforce of its predecessor.

Some earlier McLarens were a bit tricky to actually get into, but no contortions are required to slip inside the 720S's cabin through its twin-hinged dihedral doors. Once in, get comfy and buckle up for the 212-mph ride of your life.

 Performance

Top speed	212 mph
0–62 mph	2.9 secs
Power	720 hp
Torque	568 lb-ft

 Engine

Capacity	4.0-liter V8
Type	Twin turbocharged

 Efficiency

Mileage	26.4 mpg

 Dimensions

Curb weight	3,129 lb
Power/weight	460 hp/ton
Length	178.9 in

Lotus Exige Sport 380

Country of manufacture	United Kingdom		Starting at $88,500

More power, less weight, and more aerodynamic downforce – that's the Lotus way. Few cars exemplify that as well as the firm's fastest model, the Exige Sport 380, "the supercar killer." With 0–62 mph in 3.7 secs, it is as fast as some supercars with twice the Lotus's power. Carbon-fiber seats is one of its weight-saving tricks.

Small winglets at the car's sides help increase downforce, and there's also a carbon front splitter and rear diffuser to reduce pressure under the car – all very F1!

 Performance

Top speed	170 mph
0–62 mph	3.7 secs
Power	380 hp
Torque	302 lb-ft

 Engine

Capacity	3.5-liter V6
Type	Supercharged

 **Efficiency**

Mileage	27.2 mpg

 **Dimensions**

Curb weight	2,426 lb
Power/weight	313 hp/ton
Length	160.8 in

Ferrari 488 GTB

Country of manufacture	Italy	Starting at $252,800

The 488 GTB is the latest in a distinguished line of mid-engined two-seaters with beautiful curves. These have usually been courtesy of designers Pininfarina, but Ferrari did the 488 themselves. It's different in other ways too – it is the first GTB to have a turbocharged engine. It doesn't slow it down any though!

Leather dash with contrast stitching, Ferrari-red rev counter, a steering wheel that says "hold on," and a big red "Start" button – what more could you want?

 Performance

Top speed	205 mph
0–62 mph	3.0 secs
Power	670 hp
Torque	560 lb-ft

 Engine

Capacity	3.9-liter V8
Type	Twin turbocharged

 **Efficiency**

Mileage	24.8 mpg

 **Dimensions**

Curb weight	3,252 lb
Power/weight	412 hp/ton
Length	179.8 in

Aston Martin Vanquish S

Country of manufacture	United Kingdom	Starting at $266,500

James Bond would approve! The latest Vanquish S is surely his sort of car. Sitting at the top of Aston Martin's range, the 2016-revised S looks more assertive than ever, with its new carbon-fiber front splitter and rear diffuser. The V12 has been tuned to give 600 hp and has the best exhaust roar in all of motoring.

The Vanquish S is just as stunning on the inside as it is from curbside. Carbon fiber isn't just the material of choice, it is at the heart of the styling. Ever seen a center console like this before?

 Performance

Top speed	201 mph
0–62 mph	3.5 secs
Power	600 hp
Torque	465 lb-ft

 Engine

Capacity	6.0-liter V12
Type	Naturally aspirated

 **Efficiency**

Mileage	21.6 mpg

 **Dimensions**

Curb weight	3,834 lb
Power/weight	313 hp/ton
Length	186.2 in

Hypercars

▶ Supercars used to be the ultimate four-wheeled machines, but today there is a new breed at the very pinnacle of the performance spectrum – hypercars. So extreme are they that their closest rivals are pure racing cars. Like Formula 1 cars, the key to their otherworldly performance is the latest technology, with many turning to energy recovery systems (ERS) and hybrid or all-electric drivetrains to offer the most incredible speed, while active aerodynamics ensure never-before-achieved cornering abilities. Hypercars are the ultimate head turners – with the ultimate price tags!

Pagani Huayra BC

Country of manufacture	Italy	Starting at $1,400,000

Italian works of supercar art are rarely as beautifully crafted or as ferociously fast as a Pagani. First was the Zonda, then came the Huayra (*wire-ah*) that the Stig set a *Top Gear* track record with. Now there's the Huayra BC, a road car for maximum track fun, powered by a huge AMG engine with a mighty V12 roar.

The Huayra BC – the initials stand for Benny Caiola, the first person to buy a Pagani – gets a titanium exhaust that would look at home in an art gallery. The exhaust weighs just 6.4 pounds.

Performance

Top speed	238 mph
0–62 mph	2.8 secs
Power	780 hp
Torque	811 lb-ft

Engine

Capacity	6.0-liter V12
Type	Twin turbocharged

Efficiency

Mileage	Not available

 Dimensions

Curb weight	2,686 lb
Power/weight	581 hp/ton
Length	181.3 in

Porsche 918 Spyder

Country of manufacture	Germany		Starting at $845,000

The 918 Spyder is one of the cars that wrote the hypercar rulebook when it arrived in 2013. A plug-in hybrid, its V8 is supplemented by two electric motors. Heavier and not as powerful as LaFerrari or McLaren P1, it is as fast, thanks to awesome torque and all-wheel drive traction. Plus, it can do city runs on battery power alone!

Of the 918 cars Porsche made, 918 sold in just a year. To choose one of the five operating modes – Race, Sport, E, E-Power and Hybrid – there's a motorsport-type "map switch" on the steering wheel, so the driver's attention stays on the road.

 Performance

Top speed	214 mph
0–62 mph	2.6 secs
Power	887 hp
Torque	944 lb-ft

 Engine

Capacity	4.6-liter V8
Type	Gasoline/electric hybrid

 **Efficiency**

Mileage	91.1 mpg

 **Dimensions**

Curb weight	3,616 lb
Power/weight	491 hp/ton
Length	182.8 in

Koenigsegg One:1

Country of manufacture	Sweden		Starting at $2,850,000

Meet the world's first megacar! That's a car with one whole megawatt of power – in fact, just over it at 1,360 hp, in order to match the 1,360-kg weight and achieve the hypercar holy grail of a 1:1 power/weight ratio. One 2015 performance benchmark is mind-boggling: 0–200 mph in 14.3 secs – and back to naught again in just 6.0 secs!

A real Swedish stormer, and stunning to boot – assembling the body shell from 400 separate pieces takes 600 hours. Just painting one car takes between 800 and 1,200 hours, depending on the final finish.

 Performance

Top speed	250 mph (estimate)
0–62 mph	2.8 secs
Power	1,360 hp
Torque	1,011 lb-ft

 Engine

Capacity	5.0-liter V8
Type	Twin turbocharged

 **Efficiency**

Mileage	Not available

 **Dimensions**

Curb weight	3,000 lb
Power/weight	907 hp/ton
Length	177.2 in

Zenvo TS1 GT

Country of manufacture	Denmark	Starting at $1,560,000

Danish manufacturer Zenvo celebrated its first decade in 2017 with a special TS1 GT Tenth Anniversary model. Named "Sleipnir" after a Norse king's very fast eight-legged horse, it is painted Fjord Blue, with copper-bronze strips set into the bare carbon-fiber hood and roof. Like all TS1s, it is stunning and immensely powerful.

Each handmade Anniversary model interior takes 8,000 man-hours, with the copper and rhodium in the cabin switchgear costing the same as a Porsche 911's!

 Performance

Top speed	233 mph
0–62 mph	2.8 secs
Power	1,180 hp
Torque	811 lb-ft

 Engine

Capacity	5.8-liter V8
Type	Twin supercharger

 **Efficiency**

Mileage	Not available

 **Dimensions**

Curb weight	3,771 lb
Power/weight	626 hp/ton
Length	184.6 in

Hennessey Venom GT

Country of manufacture	United States	Starting at $1,600,000

Here's a real rocket ship! The Venom GT's world's fastest car claim dates from 2014 and its 270.49 mph achieved on the Space Shuttle runway at NASA's Kennedy Space Center. Another car to claim the magic 1:1 ratio, 12 of the Bugatti-beaters have been built since 2010. Next up: a Venom F5 with 300 mph targeted!

Built as both coupes and spyders, the first spyder was built for Steve Tyler from the band Aerosmith. The final edition, finished in glacier blue with white stripes, rolled out of the factory on January 17, 2017, to some lucky lead-foot collector.

 Performance

Top speed	270 mph
0–60 mph	2.7 secs
Power	1,244 hp
Torque	1,155 lb-ft

 Engine

Capacity	7.0-liter V8
Type	Twin turbocharged

 **Efficiency**

Mileage	Not available

 **Dimensions**

Curb weight	2,743 lb
Power/weight	907 hp/ton
Length	183.3 in

Bugatti Chiron

Country of manufacture	France	Starting at $3,260,000

How to replace a car like the Veyron? Easy – make it lighter and a lot more powerful! With another 500 hp over its record-breaking forebear, the Chiron will go from 0–124 mph in 6.5 secs. You need a special key to unleash its top speed, and even then, at 261 mph, it has been artificially held back for safety reasons.

Chiron's speedo is a record-breaker: it's the first to read all the way to 500 kph (310 mph). The exquisite cabin is a beautiful place from which to experience unbridled speed. Just 500 Chirons are being made.

 Performance

Top speed	261 mph
0–62 mph	2.5 secs
Power	1,500 hp
Torque	1,180 lb-ft

 Engine

Capacity	8.0-liter W16
Type	Quad turbocharged

 **Efficiency**

Mileage	22.5 mpg

 **Dimensions**

Curb weight	4,399 lb
Power/weight	682 hp/ton
Length	178.9 in

Ferrari LaFerrari

Country of manufacture	Italy		Starting at $1,416,362

The ultimate Ferrari is THE Ferrari, hence the name! It's certainly the most powerful and the fastest, with its mild hybrid kinetic energy recovery system (KERS) providing an F1-style performance boost. The 499 coupes sold out as soon as the car was unveiled – with a special 500th car selling at auction for $7 million.

The most valuable new car of the 21st century, the cockpit design layout of the LaFerrari was done in consultation with Fernando Alonso and Felipe Massa. The seat, which is modeled to the driver, is fixed in place, but the steering wheel and pedals are adjustable.

 Performance

Top speed	217 mph
0–62 mph	Sub 3.0 secs
Power	963 hp
Torque	664 lb-ft

 Engine

Capacity	6.3-liter V12
Type	Gasoline/electric hybrid

Efficiency

Mileage	20.2 mpg

 **Dimensions**

Curb weight	3,495 lb
Power/weight	551 hp/ton
Length	185.1 in

McLaren P1

Country of manufacture	United Kingdom	Starting at $1,126,000

Britain's hypercar hero since 2014, McLaren's "Ultimate Series" car is much lighter than its Porsche and Ferrari rivals. That, along with its twin-turbo V8/electric motor and active aerodynamics, gives it scintillating circuit pace. A road version of the P1 GTR has become the fastest road-registerable car at the Nürburgring.

In a race at Silverstone, the British, German, and Italian hypercars finished within 0.5 secs of each other – with the P1 first. Most appropriate as P1, inspired by F1, refers to first place. McLaren itself refers to the automaker's original founder, Bruce McLaren.

 Performance

Top speed	217 mph
0–62 mph	2.8 secs
Power	916 hp
Torque	723 lb-ft

 Engine

Capacity	3.8-liter V8
Type	Gasoline/electric hybrid

 Efficiency

Mileage	34.0 mpg

 Dimensions

Curb weight	3,076 lb
Power/weight	596 hp/ton
Length	180.6 in

Techrules Ren

Starting at $2,200,000

Chinese ingenuity meets Italian design drama in the Ren, one of the wildest hypercars yet. The electric three-seater, with its lift-up canopy like a fighter jet's, uses a small diesel turbine to charge the batteries. Techrules says it can go for 700 miles – but not if you unleash the entire 1,287 hp through all six electric motors!

Techrules plans to make just 10 of the astonishing Giugiaro-designed machines, and they will be available as single- two- or three-seaters. In the three-seater, the passengers will sit on either side of the driver, as in the McLaren F1.

Performance

Top speed	199 mph
0–62 mph	2.5 secs
Power	1,287 hp
Torque	5,753 lb-ft

Engine

Capacity	6 electric motors
Type	Turbine range extender

Efficiency

Mileage	31.5 mpg

Dimensions

Curb weight	3,594 lb
Power/weight	716 hp/ton
Length	184.8 in

Glickenhaus SCG003S

Country of manufacture	United States	Starting at $2,000,000

Jim Glickenhaus is an American car collector with a passion: to make his own race car that can match Europe's best. Now that he's made a name for himself in endurance racing, he is converting his racer into a street machine that you can drive to the store. You'll stop traffic, but there'll be nowhere to put the groceries.

The SCG003S – S for stradale or street version – has evolved from the competition car. In road-legal trim it makes few concessions, but there are more mod cons in the enticing-looking cockpit.

Performance

Top speed	217 mph
0–62 mph	3.0 secs
Power	750 hp
Torque	590 lb-ft

Engine

Capacity	4.4-liter V8
Type	Twin turbocharged

Efficiency

Mileage	Not available

Dimensions

Curb weight	2,867 lb
Power/weight	523 hp/ton
Length	189.4 in

Vanda Dendrobium

Country of manufacture	Singapore	Price unconfirmed

How's this for flower power? Unveiled at the Geneva Motor Show in 2017, the electric Dendrobium is named after a type of orchid, and the way its doors and roof open mimics the blossoming petals. It makes for a simply stunning machine. It's slated for production in 2020, so not all details are yet known.

The Dendrobium prototype, which was built by the UK's Williams Advanced Engineering company, features six-sided honeycomb-like buttons on the dash, and even the air vents, front grille, and headlight bezels repeat this motif.

 Performance

Top speed	200 mph
0–62 mph	2.7 secs (targeted)
Power	1,000 hp
Torque	Not available

 Engine

Capacity	90–100 kWh
Type	Electric motors

 **Efficiency**

Mileage	Not available

 **Dimensions**

Curb weight	3,859 lb (targeted)
Power/weight	518 hp/ton (estimate)
Length	218.1 in

NIO ep9

NextEV NIO EP9

Country of manufacture	China	Starting at $1,200,000

For a few weeks in 2017 the fastest road-registerable car at the Nürburgring Nordschleife ("Green Hell") was electric. A megawatt of power (1,342 hp) means lots of batteries and hefty weight, but with massive torque from zero revs and ace handling, this poster car of the all-electric market is an absolute scorcher!

Ten EP9s are being made at $1.48 million each. A high price tag, but then this car's carbon cockpit and chassis are designed to handle the physical demands of cornering at 3g! A jet fighter, for comparison, pulls 9g in vertical flight.

Performance

Top speed	194 mph
0–60 mph	2.7 secs
Power	1,342 hp
Torque	Not available

Engine

Capacity	4 electric motors
Type	Plug-in electric

Efficiency

Mileage	Not available

Dimensions

Curb weight	3,826 lb
Power/weight	702 hp/ton
Length	192.4 in

ItalDesign Zerouno

ItalDesign has designed some of the most successful cars in history, like the VW Golf, but never made one of its own – until now. Zerouno (No. 01) is good-looking, expensive and exclusive – just five are being made – and it's certainly fast. That's thanks to the V10 drivetrain from the Audi R8 behind the seats.

The Zerouno's interior is dominated by handcrafted carbon fiber. On the outside, racing stripes in the colors of the Italian flag run from nose to tail via the roof!

 Performance

Top speed	205 mph
0–62 mph	3.2 secs
Power	610 hp
Torque	413 lb-ft

 Engine

Capacity	5.2-liter V10
Type	Naturally aspirated

 **Efficiency**

Mileage	Not available

 **Dimensions**

Curb weight	Not available
Power/weight	Not available
Length	190.8 in

Aston Martin Valkyrie

Country of manufacture	United Kingdom	Starting at $3,200,000

The Valkyrie is the brainchild of F1 designer Adrian Newey who, with Red Bull Racing and Aston Martin, is defining a new level of road car performance. With ground-effect aerodynamics and about 1,000 hp propelling just 1,000 kg, the hybrid V12 aims to match a Le Mans winner: with 0–200 mph in an incredible 10 seconds.

Race car style for the road: that rectangular steering wheel may even be detachable, like an F1 car's, to aid entry and exit. The driving position is feet up, F1 style, while cameras replace rearview mirrors.

 Performance

Top speed	250 mph (estimate)
0–62 mph	2.0 (estimate)
Power	1,130 hp (estimate)
Torque	Not available

 Engine

Capacity	6.5-liter V12
Type	Gasoline/electric hybrid

 Efficiency

Mileage	Not available

 Dimensions

Curb weight	2,500 lb (estimate)
Power/weight	907 hp/ton (estimate)
Length	Not available

Glossary

0–60 mph/0–62 mph – a standard test to measure, in seconds, how long a car takes to accelerate from zero to 60 mph (US) or 62 mph/100 kph (Europe).

A

acceleration – a vehicle's capacity to gain speed.

aerodynamic – elements of a vehicle's shape that allows air to flow smoothly for less wind resistance.

Alcantara – durable man-made suede-like fabric.

all-wheel drive (AWD) – or 4x4, where power is transmitted to all four wheels.

B

biposto – Italian for two-seater.

biturbo – *see twin turbocharged.*

body – panels covering the car's chassis and mechanical and electrical parts.

boxer engine – or flat engine, where cylinders are horizontally opposed on either side of a crankshaft.

Boxster – used by Porsche for open top models with boxer engine built on a roadster body.

bumper – a horizontal bar at front and/or back of a car to reduce collision damage.

C

carbon fiber – a strong, lightweight carbon-fiber reinforced plastic.

cabriolet (cabrio) – a two-door car with a removable roof.

chassis – the base frame of a vehicle.

concept car – also prototype, one made to showcase new styling or technology.

convertible – a vehicle where a soft or hard roof can be opened and closed.

coupe – a sporty two-door car with a hard, fixed roof.

crossover utility vehicle (CUV) – a vehicle built on a car platform but with sport utility vehicle (SUV) features like high ground clearance.

CVT – continuously variable transmission.

Cup – model name that relates to a racing series.

curb weight – total vehicle weight including fuel, fluids and standard equipment but no passengers or load.

cylinder – a chamber in an engine in which combustion takes place. Most cars have four- six- or eight-cylinders arranged as flat/boxer (at 180° to each other), straight/inline (in a single row), V (angled away from each other) and double-V or W pattern.

D

diesel engine – where air, compressed to a high temperature in the combustion chamber, ignites the diesel fuel.

diffuser – aerodynamic feature at the rear end of a car.

downforce – or ground effect, aerodynamic design that increases vertical force and therefore grip.

drivetrain – components that generate power and transmit it to the wheels.

dual-clutch – automatic transmission with a clutch for even-numbered gears and one for odd-numbered gears.

E

efficiency – how far a car will travel on a unit (imperial gallon) of fuel.

electric vehicle (EV) – uses energy stored in rechargeable batteries to drive electric motors.

electronic stability system – computerized technology to improve a car's traction.

engine – where chemical energy in a fuel is converted to mechanical energy in order to turn a shaft.

engine size (capacity) – measured in liters or cubic inches or centimeters (cu-in or cc), it is the volume of air sucked in by all the pistons as they move from top to bottom of the cylinders.

exhaust – piping that carries the gases produced during combustion to the rear of the car.

F

factory tuned – a model that has engine or chassis upgrades done by the manufacturer. Often indicated in the model name, like Mercedes-AMG, BMW M or Cadillac V-series.

flat engine – *see boxer engine.*

front-wheel drive – where power is directed only to the front wheels.

four-wheel drive (4WD) – *see all-wheel drive.*

G

gasoline engine – fuel is ignited by a spark in the combustion chamber.

gearbox – or transmission or 'box, a metal box containing toothed cogs that are engaged manually, via a clutch and gear selector, or automatically to increase or decrease speed.

grille – an opening at the front of a car so air can pass to the radiator.

GT – Grand Touring or Gran Turismo; a high performance car.

GTB – Grand Tourer Berlinetta; a coupe-style GT.

GTI (GTi) – Grand Tourer Injection; a car with a fuel-injected engine.

GTR (GT-R) – Gran Turismo Racing.

GTS – Gran Turismo Spider (convertible), Sport (four-door sedan) or Special.

H

handling – how a vehicle steers, and its maneuverability on corners.

hatchback (hatch) – a car with a full-width opening at the rear.

horsepower (hp) – the unit of measurement for engine power. Originally used to express the power of a steam locomotive in terms of the strength of draft horses.

HSV – Holden Special Vehicles.

hybrid – a vehicle that has a battery-powered electric motor and a fuel-powered engine.

K

kilowatt hour (kWh) – measure of the electric energy produced (or consumed) in an hour.

L

LED – light-emitting diode.

Le Mans – 24-hour endurance car race held in Le Mans, France.

length – measured in inches (in) from the most forward-facing point of a car to its most rear-facing point.

LS – Luxury Sedan.

M

marque – another word for "make of car."

megacar – a car that has more than one megawatt (mW) or 1,340 hp of power.

mileage – or consumption or fuel economy, the distance a vehicle can travel on one unit of fuel. Tests to measure this vary between countries, but cover highway or city driving. A combined figure covers highway and city conditions. For all-electric cars, the mpg is a combustion engine equivalent.

miles per gallon (mpg) – miles traveled on an imperial gallon of fuel.

muscle car – American and Australian term for a high-performance car.

N

naturally aspirated – when air intake into the engine is determined only by atmospheric pressure.

NSX – New Sportscar eXperimental.

Nürburgring – an old car racetrack in Germany. Nordschleife (known as "Green Hell"), the north circuit, is now used mainly by manufacturers which test their powerful models there and aim to set the fastest lap times.

O

oversteer – when the rear tires skid and the car turns into a corner more than the amount intended.

P–Q

paddle shift – *see semi-automatic transmission.*

pillar – vertical or near vertical supports on a car, for example: A-pillars are either side of the windshield; B-pillars, behind the front doors; C-pillars, behind the rear doors.

piston – a component that moves up and down inside a cylinder.

power – *see horsepower.*

power to weight (hp/ton) – correlation between the power (hp) of an engine to the car's curb weight (ton).

production car – a mass-produced car for sale to the public and road legal.

quattro – Italian for four, and meaning four-wheel drive (Audi) or four-door (Maserati).

R

R – may indicate Race specification in a car's model name.

RA – Race Applicant.

redline – a red line on a car's rev counter (tachometer) that indicates maximum engine speed expressed as revolutions per minute.

revolutions per minute (rpm) – how many times per minute engine components, like the crankshaft, rotate.

roadster – a two-seater car with a folding roof.

RS – Rally Sport or Racing Sport.

S

sedan – a medium-to-large fixed-roof, four-door car.

semi-automatic transmission (SAT) – gearbox where gears are chosen manually, but the clutch is automatic

sequential gearbox – a manual transmission where gears are selected by clicking a button, not moving a gear stick. Common on race cars.

SL – Sports Light or Series Limited.

speed – the rate at which a car moves, and also refers to the number of forward gear ratios, as in five- or six-speed, in the gearbox.

speed limiter – a device that limits a car's top speed. Some manufacturers, mostly European, limit their fastest models to 155 mph.

spider (spyder) – a car with a removable roof.

splitter – aerodynamic feature at the front of the car.

spoiler – aerodynamic device to increase downforce by "spoiling" the airflow over the car.

sports car – a small, powerful two-seater car.

SRT – Street & Racing Technology (Fiat Chrysler).

ST - Sports Technologies (Ford).

stradale – Italian for "road going," and usually indicates a road legal version of a track car.

straight or inline – *see cylinder.*

supercharger – an engine driven device that forcibly compresses air into the cylinders to increase power.

suspension – springs, dampers and anti-sway bars that maximize friction between tires and road for handling, steering and comfort.

Sport Utility Vehicle (SUV) – a high-riding vehicle with a large opening at the rear.

SV – Special Version.

switchgear – the switches and electric controls in a car.

T

targa – a semi-convertible car where a section of roof can be removed.

throttle – another name for the accelerator pedal, and also for the system that controls the volume of air entering the engine.

trim – the materials, like wood, leather or metals, used to cover or decorate the interior of a car.

torque – the force generated by an engine to rotate the crankshaft at a given speed.

transmission – *see gearbox.*

turbocharger – an exhaust-gas driven turbine (fan) that forces air into the engine to increase power.

twin turbocharged – or biturbo, a car with two turbochargers.

U–W

understeer – when the front tires skid and the car turns into a corner less than the amount intended.

V – this indicates an engine where the cylinders are arranged in a V-shape on either side of the crankshaft.

valves per cylinder – the number of intake and exhaust valves in a cylinder.

venturi – an aerodynamic effect underneath a car.

VXR – race track-styled road car with high performance (Vauxhall).

W – an engine where cylinders are in banks resembling the letter W. For example, W16 with 16 cylinders.

wagon – a large car with rear opening into a luggage/storage area.

Index